Reginald Heber Howe

On the Birds Highway

Reginald Heber Howe

On the Birds Highway

ISBN/EAN: 9783744666633

Printed in Europe, USA, Canada, Australia, Japan

Cover: Foto ©Thomas Meinert / pixelio.de

More available books at **www.hansebooks.com**

"OUR FRIENDS THE CHICKADEES."

ON THE BIRDS' HIGHWAY

BY

REGINALD HEBER HOWE, Jr.

With Photographic Illustrations by the Author and a Frontispiece in Color from a Painting by
LOUIS AGASSIZ FUERTES

BOSTON
SMALL, MAYNARD & COMPANY
1899

TO MY

MOTHER AND FATHER

THIS BOOK

IS LOVINGLY INSCRIBED

Preface

It is my hope that these little Sketches may lead others to enjoy all that I have enjoyed "On the Birds' Highway."

The appendix contains a number of lists of birds from those localities treated in the body of the book, which may be of some value to field ornithologists.

I wish to thank Mr. Louis Agassiz Fuertes for his great kindness in presenting me with the frontispiece, the Editors of the Boston "Commonwealth" and "Transcript" for their permission to reprint a number of the chapters which have appeared in their papers, and also many other friends for kind assistance in various ways.

REGINALD HEBER HOWE, Jr.

Longwood, Massachusetts,
April, 1899.

Contents.

Chap.		Page
I.	Winter Birds	1
II.	December by Land and Sea	12
III.	On the Sands of Ipswich	20
IV.	Among the Foothills	29
V.	Where February is Spring	44
VI.	Familiar and Unfamiliar Bird Songs	55
VII.	In the Mount Hope Lands	69
VIII.	Under the Shadow of Wachusett	78
IX.	A Meadow Chronicle	91
X.	Swallow Pond	99
XI.	In the Land of Norumbega	107
XII.	Summer Birds	114
XIII.	Along the Beach	121
XIV.	Late Summer in the Adirondacks	134
APPENDIX.	Local Lists	153
	BRISTOL, R. I.	
	HUBBARDSTON, MASS.	
	CHATEAUGAY LAKE, N. Y.	

List of Illustrations

Full-page

	PAGE
Chickadees	*Frontispiece*
Mount Hope on Narragansett Bay	13
The Ipswich Dunes	21
The Presidential Range	28
Rock Creek	45
American Robin (from painting)	54
An Osprey's Nest	68
Mount Wachusett	79
A Meadow Clearing	90
Swallow Pond	98
Islesborough	106
A Beach Opening	115
The Atlantic	120
The Camp at the Spring	135

Marginals

Screech Owls (from life)	2
Red-shouldered Hawk	4
Loon	6
Lapland Longspur	8

LIST OF ILLUSTRATIONS

	PAGE
Northern Shrike with Redpoll	10
Myrtle Warbler	15
Short-eared Owl	18
American Herring Gull	24
Red-bellied Nuthatch	32
Hudson Bay Chickadee	34
Red-breasted Merganser	40
Cardinal	47
Mourning Dove	51
Turkey Vulture	52
Song Sparrow	58
White-throated Sparrow	59
American Woodcock	61
Phœbe (from life)	64
Downy Woodpecker's Nest (*in situ*)	70
Belted Kingfisher	73
American Robin on Nest (from life)	81
Kingbird's Nest (*in situ*)	83
Towhee	86
Green Heron	87
Baltimore Oriole's Nest	93
American Crow (from life)	101
Black-crowned Night Heron	103
Sparrow Hawk	109
Snowy Owl	111
American Golden-eye	113
Bobolink	118
Spotted Sandpiper's Nest (*in situ*)	122
Wilson's Tern	124
Wilson's Tern's Nest (*in situ*)	126

	PAGE
Least Tern	128
Bank Swallow	130
Laughing Gull	131
Heath Hen	132
Bald Eagle	137
Great Blue Heron	138
Canadian Warbler	139
Work of Pileated Woodpecker	141
Semipalmated Plover	143
Barred Owl	148
American Three-toed Woodpecker	149

On the Birds' Highway

I

WINTER BIRDS

THE sky is gray, a few great snow-flakes are softly falling on the autumn-painted leaves ; it is the first storm of the winter, and, as the flakes grow thicker and thicker and the shadows of a November afternoon stretch out their dusky fingers across the whitening ground, another year's foliage is laid to rest. The sun is a tardy riser now and the birds tardy risers too. How changed the woodland as we stand looking out across the meadow to the woods! The earth has donned her polar robes and greets the fiery sun immaculate. Shall we break that even mantle, pierced by weeds and scarred only by birds' and mammals' tread? If we are to wish our friends good morning, we must, though as we part the virgin snow we feel we are intruding and wish to walk bareheaded into Nature's sanctum — winter woods.

Let us first greet our resident friends and then the visitors — though perhaps it would be more polite to welcome the weary travellers first.  We have ploughed our way scarcely a dozen yards when from among the sere weeds we catch the sweet notes of a flock of goldfinches. They have donned their winter garments too and are gleaning a morning meal in truly boreal style. A flock of crows flap slowly by, their dark shadows on the snow betraying them. They are wanderers now and must depend for their livelihood on the beach where the kind ocean leaves its bounty or on orchard or field where ungathered apples, corn and vegetables can be mined in the snow.

We have reached a thicket of cat brier with alders bordering it, and hear

> "a tiny voice hard by,
> Gay and polite, a cheerful cry,
> Chic-chicadeedee; saucy note
> Out of sound heart and merry throat."

Of course this joyful little fellow who sings his name from one year's end to the other is an old friend of all of us, and as he scurries about,

> "Hurling defiance at vast death;
> This scrap of valor just for play
> Fronts the north-wind in waistcoat gray,"

we read fearlessness in his twinkling eye and warm friendship in his actions. From this protecting patch of growth appears another sweet-voiced bird — the song sparrow; later in the day while the winter is young and when the sun remembers its summer friends we may hear him singing softly to himself — singing of the spring to be.

A few minutes more and we are in the woods, bare now but beautiful, for we see the grace of their many arms, which seem to be imploring the north wind that rattles them so cruelly to give them back their leaves of which it has just stripped them. As we are welcomed from the alders and birches by the chickadee we are welcomed to the woods by the blue jay, who stands with acorn in his claw shouting loudly his imitation of the red-shouldered hawk between each savage peck at the nut.

> "His character a tonic,
> His future a dispute;
> Unfair an immortality
> That leaves this neighbor out."

What was that nasal "quank" that interrupted the jay's performance? It is the white-breasted nuthatch climbing head down upon an old pine stump; he must have little blood in his veins, especially if he sleeps upside down as it is hinted, or he would have apoplexy and might wear a scarlet patch on his head as does the male downy woodpecker who is hitching like a respectable bird up a neighboring maple stub. We have met one of those merry parties that always go hand in hand through the winter woods. There is the nuthatch and downy and a number of chickadees and the monotonous brown creeper is climbing his spiral ladder about an oak, and from a patch of young spruces we hear the clear note of the golden-crowned kinglets, fearless little sparks of life and true acrobats. Where the path runs down the hillside to the brook we flush a ruffed grouse from the underbrush and, when the rising "whir" is over, with set wings he sails off through the birches and is gone. A flock of winter robins are feeding on the vermilion berries of the black alder by the brook and to hear their glad shout is worth our long walk through the snow.

Returning by another route over a bare hill where the snow has drifted against the wall we find in each gap between the stones or in the gate-ways the tracks of chipmunk[1] and mice. Something has walked the top of the old wall too, for on each white-capped boulder four toes have pressed, for which Bob White is probably responsible.

The snow has many a story to tell as we tramp along: a rabbit has taken a turn about his "brier patch," squirrels have wandered in the woods, and a crow

---

[1] As far as my experience goes, the chipmunk is only dormant in the very coldest weather of the winter.

has crossed our path. From a few scattered apple trees we hear the flicker calling. These old trees are his best winter friends and supply him with both food and lodgings. The downy loves the gnarled limbs also; but his cousin the hairy, at least about the more settled country, prefers deeper woods.

It will pay us to make a circuit through the cedars before we cross the marsh and the bridge, for the only common winter warbler, the yellow rump — and he is rare enough, — often spends his long winter days among their friendly embrace. If he is here, he is very disobliging this forenoon. We do not even see a blue jay about the old hut; if we were farther north we would certainly see the other jay, — the moose bird, by the door.

The marsh is cold and drear now; the storm has left, however, great patches of grass uncovered and the meadow lark is difficult to flush to wing into the biting air and settles down in the nearest cover without a note. There is no loon in sight either up or down the river to-day, although at times through the winter when it is open we may catch a glimpse of one floating on its icy waters.

Toward sunset we may hear the "quawk" of a night heron as he flies over, or at the fireside be startled by the whinny of a screech or the hoot of a barred owl perched on a dead stub and whose outline is traced against the cold moonlight of a winter's sky.

> "Or Arctic creature, dimly stirred
> By tropic hint, — some travelled bird
> Imported to the wood.

Far back in September, when the summer foliage was just changing to its autumn splendor, we welcomed our first northern winter visitor, the snow bird, and on throughout the cold season he will be one of our closest friends and we shall bid him farewell in early May with regret although his place be filled with many a gayer songster. We met on our ramble the brown creeper who is really a visitor from the north, and beyond the very few that spend the summer with us here in certain localities in Massachusetts, the majority do not arrive within our woods until October.

If we were to go to the beaches, dunes or meadows along the shores during the winter, especially in the early or latter part, we would find running hither and thither a jolly company of shore larks with their comrades the snow buntings and perhaps a stray lapland longspur. They are all beautiful birds, and as they wheel up and down or dodge between the driftwood their plumage is displayed to the best advantage; the larks with yellow breasts and black collars, the buntings, "snowflakes" as they are called, but like snowflakes fallen on the earth where winter sunshine shows small dark patches through.

Another guest from boreal regions, one that makes your heart glad with his sweet low song in midwinter from out the thicket, is the tree sparrow and many a bleak day this chestnut-crowned pedestrian and the chickadee have been my only companions.

On Christmas day last year while making my way over log and brook, a little brown bird whirled from my feet and bobbed out of sight behind a log. A rare bird here in late December and January, I thought, as the saucy winter wren appeared around the end of the old log. The chickadee's cousin, the Hudson Bay tit, I have never met with on my tramps in this locality, but he has made flying trips to all three of the southern New England States and I hope to meet him soon on the birds' highway.

Those birches which but yesterday stood above the immaculate snow with buds intact, are now alive with redpolls who shower us and the snow with thousands of calyces as they rob the trees of their tender buds; fearless, dear little fluffy fellows and typical birds of a winter scene. In yonder hemlocks and among the sere "stick tight" weeds at their foot a flock of siskins or pine finches are feeding and are murmuring their glad notes for the season. On our morning tramp we may meet the brigand shrike who is in the act of impaling a song sparrow or goldfinch on a thorn or in a wild chase after a junco. Although a murderer he is interesting — murderers always interest the public — and yet late in March we may hear his mocking-bird-like song echoing from the thicket, a true musical performance that at our first meeting we would have hardly credited to his bloodthirsty throat.

Wandering, erratic, welcome travellers, here to-day, to-morrow many miles to the north or southward, are the crossbills; one may find them stripping the larches or pines in our woodland, as complacently as if they had been there all their lives, in any month of the year, though their home is in the great coniferous forests of the north. Curious birds, and if only obliging as they often are, one can watch them shell the cones with their singular bills, so well adapted to their work.

It is one of those still biting mornings in January when the sun makes no impression on the snow-drift. We are standing by a clump of pines on a hillside scanning the snow-bound country, our hands thrust deep into our pockets, when with the quickness of thought we are carried back to September when we sat alert in our marsh blind calling the passing yellow-legs down to our decoys. There is a chorus of plaintive whistles from the heavens; then with a "whir" a flock of pine grosbeaks alight amid the pines. Among the chrome yellow marked young males and females we catch sight of a few exquisite rosy adult males. They have arrived, they are everywhere in the elms, spruces and barberry bushes. The incessant crackling of their bills as they split bud after bud, or the chaff on the ground betrays their presence. You might have tramped many a mile yesterday and not have seen a bird, but they have come in the night by hundreds, dropping out of a clear sky.

The sun is sinking slowly in the west, the bleak March wind is driving song sparrow and junco to cover and the great oaks stand out against the tinted sky. This last fierce battle of winter does not suggest the awaking of spring on the morrow but the next moon will shine on a new world,

"while, through the veins of the earth, riots the ichor of Spring."

II

DECEMBER BY LAND AND SEA

DOWN one of the muddy rain-soaked roads of an old Rhode Island town I splashed, as the southwest wind drove the cold drizzle of a December's storm against my face. There are lessons to be learned in all weathers out-of-doors, and Nature puts on new aspects for each phase of the heavens. The roadside was aflame in places with the vermilion berries of the black alder, the dark crimson spires of the sumac gave another bit of color to the foreground. The waters of Narragansett Bay were leaden save for a few waves that foamed into white caps on the further shore. Mount Hope was wrapped in mist as were the Tiverton and the Rhode Island hills. Although the hollows were piled with the glory of the autumn woods, there was a great deal of color still warming the winter landscape with its ruddy glow.

MOUNT HOPE ON NARRAGANSETT BAY.

The rain seemed to have brought out the colors of fallen leaf, twig, and meadow. The tops of the young birches looked smoky and purple, the orange shoots of the willows stood out against the gray woods, the bay bushes of the fallow land were silvery and gave light to the cedars they stood over against on the hill.

A migration of crows flew in wavering line from the woods on the western slope of the Mount in a southwesterly course, beating into the storm all day long. Hundreds must have passed over during the hours of daylight. By a wayside pond I started a flock 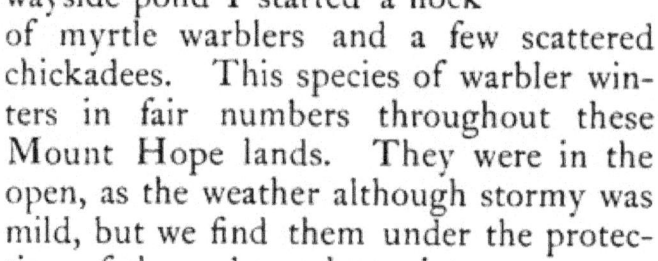 of myrtle warblers and a few scattered chickadees. This species of warbler winters in fair numbers throughout these Mount Hope lands. They were in the open, as the weather although stormy was mild, but we find them under the protection of the cedars when winter rages.

As I entered a strip of dark oak woods, where last summer I gathered the death-like flowers of the Indian pipe, the wind hauled to the northwest and a great dark cloud poured down rain and wind, swinging the coasting schooner that lay at anchor in mid-stream in a twinkling, and making the woods roar and crack with its fury. A rift in the nimbus clouds followed the squall and the sun broke through and bathed in light the Tiverton hills. What a change had taken place! The undergrowth sparkled in the sunlight and the sheep that had huddled together in the right angle of a wall began to crop the jewelled stubble. As the heavens were cleared of the dark clouds, the bay, a great mirror of the sky, began to reflect its glorious blue and against the scurrying storm a faint rainbow hung over the Mount.

Three flickers left the eaves of a haycap roof as I passed and a single herring gull sailed back and forth over the shining waters of the transformed Narragansett. Among the tall ungathered, but still green, cabbages of the garden a song sparrow lisped; his summer environment had slowly faded away until only the box hedge, the cabbages and the bare bean poles remained; but the hedge gave forth its same delicious fragrance notwithstanding he did not pipe his song.

As the few wisps of clouds in the western sky were tinged with pink, winter gull after winter gull appeared out of the blood-red afterglow and floated out over the waters of the bay. The sky line in the east was a vivid purplish hue, while above it, glowed the reflected exquisite pink of the higher western heavens.

On the eleventh I took the beach road out of the then deserted and quiet town of Newport. There were no bathers except a few coot and an old loon that floated just outside the surf. I followed the edge of the shale around Easton's Point. A dozen or more coasting schooners were scudding to the southward under a fresh nor'west breeze. A square-rigger was hull down far off Cormorant Rock and West Island Light loomed up beyond Sachuest Point. A few red-necked and horned grebes were swimming about the rocks and two red-breasted mergansers flew out to sea. A few "beds" of coot lay off shore a mile or so. The ocean looked just as it does in summer save for the absence of sandpipers — for not even a purple was to be seen — and for the presence of the grebes and other sea-fowl. Rounding the point, I entered the sand dunes back of the second beach in hope of seeing a short-eared or snowy owl. Hanging Rock stood out against the sky, a bold bit of Nature's stonework.  Bishop Berkeley is said to have written his sermons in the hollow of this rock; it stands two hundred yards back of the beach with the dunes stretching between; we find among the Bishop's writings that the ocean broke at his feet and the sandhills that to-day roll to its base are evidence of the truth of his words. Not an owl did we meet in the dunes, or a snow bunting or a shore lark on our way back along the beach.

Among the junipers in the steep eastern slope of Mount Hope, where the wind did not reach and the sun lay, on the morning of the twelfth, three crossbills wandered and a flock of myrtle warblers "chucked" as I stumbled through the underbrush. Terrace after terrace of quartz robed in moss formed the descent to the clearing.

Rhode Island looked as lovely and peaceful as ever, although its fields were sere, its woodlands brown ; the junipers and the bay gave it its striking colors. Nature never offends the eye, we never fault or dislike the coloring of a sunset, criticise a landscape, or any child of Nature. Perfect, with all its variety, it comes from the hand of Him who made it.

III

ON THE SANDS OF IPSWICH

A FIVE-MILE drive in the early morning of a winter's day over rolling country, with few trees to offer any protection from the bleak winds, in a rickety buggy drawn by a still more rickety horse, with two other occupants of its narrow seat beside yourself, does not sound attractive, to say the least. The shay, if you so choose to call it, had a decided "flavor of mild decay," and I must say I thought the hour named for its ruin was near at hand, if it did not arrive *en route*. The only object of interest on the road was an extremely small building pointed out to us by our driver as the only schoolhouse in the locality. A "regular knowledge box" he called it. Reaching the last summit, the dunes lay before us to the east, one wind-tossed ocean of sand; to the north the Ipswich and to the south the Essex River emptied into the dark,

THE IPSWICH DUNES.

gray Atlantic, while between us and the dunes stretched a broad salt marsh, dotted with duck blinds, to the sea.

The white tower of Ipswich Light rose from among the sandhills, and beyond Bug Light stood on the crest of a dune. Our journey ended at a quaint old house on the shores of the Essex River, surrounded on all sides by the shifting sands. Having deposited our luggage in a room whose floor shelved in every direction possible, though anything even or level here would have looked strange and unnatural, we started for the beach beyond the dunes. Herring gulls crowded the uncovered bars by the hundreds, and now and then a few ducks would fly low over the water, passing from one feeding ground to another.

The bare ribs of a wreck protruded from the shore, the keel having long ago been buried by the encroaching sands. Large flocks of snow buntings hopped over the seaweed or sat muffled up on the driftwood, and when startled would fly farther down the beach, uttering a chorus of short, sharp notes. Shore larks also were numerous here, running around tufts of stubble; they are generally to be found in company with the former species. One of the most noticeable features of these dunes are the myriads of tracks, both of bird and mammal, that trace their surfaces. Crows, gulls, larks and buntings could be followed by their footprints; and skunks, too, had done some midnight hunting, while the small tracks of field mice marked their wandering about the sand.

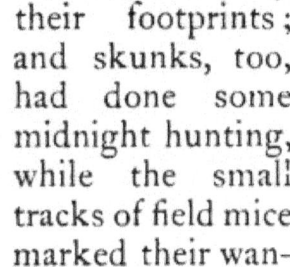

Small patches of stunted firs and cranberry grew in the hollows between the hills, giving color to the landscape, and the ridges themselves were covered with a thin growth of yellow grasses (*Ammophila arenaria*), the seed tassels of which were eagerly sought for by the larks and bunting. Great flocks of crows crossed and recrossed the neck, cawing incessantly. Four meadow larks were seen several times during the afternoon on the marshlands of the Essex River. Gaining the summit of the highest dune we watched the sun set behind the hills toward Ipswich, and the fourteenth of December was a day of the past.

At half-past five o'clock on the following morning we made our way out on to the moonlit sandhills, whose weird undulating outlines were yet indistinct in the growing light; occasionally we would catch a glimpse of Ipswich Light toward the north, gilding the highest dunes. Standing in a pit dug the day before in the sand, we waited to see what the advancing dawn would bring us of interest. The tide was far out, and the breaking of waves on the distant, unseen bar, the crying of gulls and the cawing of passing crows sounded wild and uncanny. It was terribly cold. By half-past six o'clock the east was all aglow, and at seven the sun appeared above Cape Ann. A large flock of buntings flew restlessly about far up the beach, and two horned larks played their game of hide and seek around the tufts of withered grass. We saw nothing of the Ipswich sparrows. Following the path that runs back to the house we heard the call of a solitary flicker, — certainly a strange place for him to be spending the winter.

There were no red crossbills among the firs, but the modest song of a tree sparrow often broke the silence.

At nine o'clock we left the dunes behind us, white-capped by the touch of the morning sun.

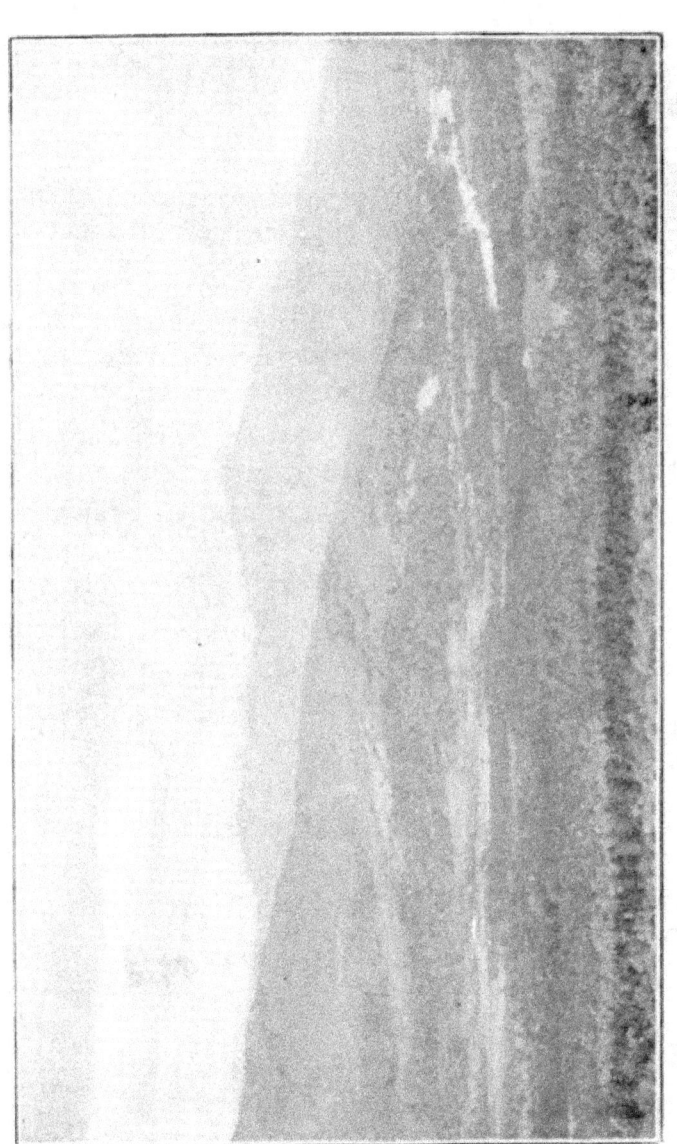

The Presidential Range.

IV

AMONG THE FOOTHILLS

WE left Boston from the Union Station *via* the western division of the Boston and Maine Railroad at one on the afternoon of December the twenty-sixth. We were bound northward for Shelburne, New Hampshire, a small town, consisting of some twenty-eight farms, on the Androscoggin River, about two miles from the Maine and sixty from the Canadian border.

The sky was gray, foreboding rain or snow. From the car window the passing country looked bare and monotonous. Second growth white and pitch pine, birch and a few scattered hemlock composed the passing woodland panorama. Over the Merrimac a single herring gull was flying and large flocks of crows were feeding in the meadows. After crossing the Saco River we began to notice small patches of snow lying in the shaded corners and hollows; even the smallest brooks, however, were open and running merrily. Just at dusk we arrived at Old Orchard Beach; the surf was breaking upon the sands and the Atlantic looked cold, ashen and forbidding. A change of cars was necessary at Portland, where we crossed to the Grand Trunk Station. Standing on the platform, we looked out over Casco Bay. Only a few of its three hundred and sixty-five islands were visible through the darkness, for night had shut down in earnest. After another troublesome change of cars at Lewiston Junction we reached Shelburne at half after eight o'clock and were met by Mr. B—— in a double mountain wagon.

The farm lay but a mile across the Androscoggin River, but as the ice was running we were obliged to drive three miles or so up the valley, cross the only bridge over the river near Shelburne, and drive back down the valley to the farm. When the river is solid with ice or fordable as in summer, the drive from the station is about one mile instead of seven. It was drizzling and the road was ankle deep in mud. The horses took us galloping up one hill and down the next, bringing distant mist-covered foothills in view. We reached the farm at last and after a hearty supper turned in for the night, while the wind roared about the house and drove the rain in sheets against the window panes.

" The wintry west extends his blast,
 And hail and rain does blaw;
Or, the stormy north sends driving forth
 The blinding sleet and snaw."

When we peered from our window before sunrise the wind was blowing half a gale from the westward, driving rain across the meadows of the valley and snow higher up upon the hills, a far from promising sight. However, by half after eight o'clock blue patches of sky appeared overhead and the base of the distant foothills became visible. An hour later, the sky had almost cleared and we started out across a small clearing and up a lumber road, down which a small brook from the hills above came tumbling over fallen logs and stones. Half way up the hillside we reached a deserted lumber camp, an odd affair built of logs and roofed with rough boards, the chinks filled with grasses. We pushed on farther up the hillside, and entered another lumber road running along the brow of a ridge. Usnea "moss" hung from the great spruces, and the beautifully white boles of the canoe-birch made the woods a scene of striking grandeur and beauty. Here we met a flock of chickadees and red-bellied nuthatches. A little farther up the road we found a small flock of crossbills feeding among the cones at the top of the spruces.

The woods about Shelburne are of mixed growth; white, Norway and pitch pine, spruce, canoe and yellow birch, beech, ash, balsam fir, hemlock and red oak are the most common species; in fact, Shelburne is noted for its variety of trees.

After following along the ridge, we began to descend again into the valley. Looking out over the tree-tops below us, the mist-hung sides of Mounts Moriah and Winthrop were seen to the southward. Leaving the woods, we tramped out over the meadows along the Androscoggin and started a large flock of snow buntings containing at least fifty individuals, from the ploughed ground. The wind blew furiously, taking one nearly off one's feet, and, catching the buntings as soon as they took wing, swept them like snowflakes before us.

In the afternoon we again set out, this time toward the eastward and along the main road, but we met no birds of any kind. On the shores of a pond at the foot of Crow's Nest Mountain, great clumps of pitcher plants were growing, their tubular leaves filled to the brim with ice-cold water. One must go into the deep woods and follow the lumber-roads to find bird life in the winter season. During the morning we heard and saw many red squirrels, but the grays were entirely absent.

After we returned, sitting at my window I looked over the valley toward the south, across the Androscoggin from whose opposite banks rose the foothills of Mount Moriah. Olivet was in the foreground and Mount Moriah itself towered 4500 feet above and behind it, while fifteen miles to the southwest the base of Mount Madison and at intervals its peak, the sharpest within view, and that of Mount

Adams beyond, appeared from out the white, fleecy clouds that enveloped them. Mount Madison is 5759 feet above the level of the sea and Mount Adams 5700 feet. The sun went down behind the foothills at about half after three o'clock, tinging the scurrying clouds with golden light; and the rolling outline of the foothills stood sharply out against the fading light of a mid-winter sky. Great cakes of ice covered the banks of the river, giving a touch of white to the gray lowlands and in seeming contrast to the then black rolling hills.

The sky was covered on the morning of the twenty-eighth with dark clouds, rifts only now and then visible; Mount Moriah, the highest mountain not under cloud, was in full view before us. We had planned a trip, the night before, to visit a lumber camp some six miles back in the woods; we left the farm at about half after eight o'clock bound thither. Our guide led us to the north-westward toward Bald Cap Mountain, at whose base the camp was situated. Striking across a small clearing, we found the path, marked by blazes along the side of Mount Ingalls. Chickadees were numerous, but their Hudson Bay cousins were nowhere to be seen. Deer tracks were occasionally found and a few red or white winged crossbills were feeding in the tops of the spruces. Many ice-fringed brooks came tumbling down from above as we tramped along the hillside. " He sendeth the springs into the valleys, which run among the hills," and they seemed to be doing their best to follow out the Scriptural teaching.

We paused for a moment to look off over the valley. The clouds had somewhat lifted, Mounts Moriah, Adams, and Madison were visible to their summits, but Mount Washington was still enveloped in cloud about half-way down its sides. Just before joining a logging road, we started a partridge from among the fallen birch logs. Following the path up the gulch, we crossed Mill Brook, and off through the trees we could see where it plunged over a cliff on the side of Bald Cap. Reaching the lumber camp, we found horse-shoeing going on. We also learned to our regret that the Canada jay, during the thaw about a week before, had disappeared, probably going back farther into the woods toward Lake Umbagog. We remained at this camp but a few minutes and then retraced our steps to another, farther back down the gorge, owned by our guide. This camp proved to be a smaller one, consisting of three log huts, a stable, out-house, and bunk and cook room. Only three of the lumbermen had returned from their Christmas vacation. The dinner we partook of there, was the only thing I do not care to remember about my Shelburne trip. Darkness pervaded the room, but I remember seeing the following articles of food, of which I ate most sparingly: wretched beef, black potatoes, leaden biscuit, and molasses, all served in dirty tin dishes in the most uninviting manner. I felt relieved on leaving this camp, and wished its occupants joy during the coming winter. I inwardly felt that for me to remain there meant starvation.

After regaining the logging road our guide left us to return to the farm by the quickest route, and we sauntered along in hope of seeing more bird-life. A few scattered flocks of crossbills, large companies of chickadees and golden-crowned kinglets infested the pines. My companion decided to brave the waters of Mill Brook and disappeared in the pines on the opposite bank. I had worn moccasins and the rough walking had made me somewhat footsore, so leaving the gorge and its lumber camps I made the road and started homeward, seeing but two blue jays during the walk.

The trees that are felled on the foothills are of the following varieties and used for the purposes named: Spruce, which is crushed and used for paper making; yellow birch and rock maple for bobbins; hemlock for planks; and canoe birch for spools; and the bark of the hemlock is also shipped by rail for tannin.

It was not until the morning of the twenty-ninth that we were able to see the summit of Mount Washington. The sky was then clear and a hoar frost covered the meadows and pine branches. Tramping up an old lumber road on the hillside behind the farm, we obtained a splendid view of the Presidential Range,

Mount Madison in the foreground, Adams, Jefferson, Clay and Washington rising in order behind it. The peak a short distance down the side of Washington was snowbound.

A few crossbills, two blue jays and a merry company of chickadees, red and white breasted nuthatch, were among the spruces. The little red squirrels were very numerous, and so tame that when my companion made a squeaking sound they approached within a few feet of us, their bright eyes twinkling and their bodies twitching with nervous excitement. We passed a deserted lumber camp and flushed a " partridge " from some hemlock boughs about its dooryard. The loud tattooing of a woodpecker attracted us and we soon found a female hairy and three downies about a few old stubs. The difference in size between these two species is quite noticeable when the birds are seen together. We returned to the farm down the old logging road. Great piles of hemlock bark and corded wood ran along each side of the path, and again a grouse sprang from the thicket and whirred into denser cover.

In the afternoon we tramped up another lumber road toward Mount Ingalls. One is struck, in wandering through the woods on these foothills, with the variety of trees and mosses. I could name but few of the mosses, but there were some of lovely yellow and silver color and texture, and a curious burnt-looking moss clung to the boulders. Evergreen was also plentiful, and "peat-moss" grew in patches through the woods. The nuthatches were everywhere, as in the morning, and the difference between the notes of the two species was quite marked, the red-breasted being yan, yan, yan, repeated often so many times that you wonder when the bird takes breath; the white-breasted had a longer quank, quank.

It seemed to be our fortune to meet hairy woodpeckers on the twenty-ninth, for on entering an old apple orchard back of one of the farms, a male was climbing about a small tree. Higher up in the woods we saw another male, and when returning a young male was tapping on the posts of a log fence, while in a small clearing the mournful whistle of a red crossbill caught my ear. He was flying over toward the south, and the rays of the setting sun behind the mountains lighted up his bright red plumage so that he fairly seemed to burn.

Anchor ice formed during the night of the twenty-eighth and ninth on the bottom of the Androscoggin, so that a canoe trip had to be given up. Just before dark a sheldrake passed, flying east down the river valley; as long as the river remains open, one may now and then see this species about Shelburne.

When the snow is deep upon the mountains, the deer feed upon the boughs of the hubble-bush and young birch; we found during our tramps trees and bushes off which they had dined. Small flocks of pine siskins were heard twice along the edge of the clearings.

On the last day of our visit we again went up the same logging road back of the farm. As usual, by the camp we started a grouse, and among the spruces the nuthatches, chickadees, and kinglets were very numerous. With a birch call

—that is, a thin piece of paper birch-bark stretched between two small sticks — I brought a half dozen blue jays in the trees above our heads, where they bobbed about screaming, with open beak and quivering wings. How I wished they were Canada jays!

A few crossbills crossed the sky above the spruces. These crossbills I found far from tame; in fact, so wild that but in one instance was I sure which species they were. Perhaps the mildness of the weather was the cause of their unsociability. The Presidential Range could be seen splendidly that morning. A discovery that puzzled me a good deal when walking up the logging road down which were the frozen waters of a brook, was that from the bottom half way up the hillside the ice remained hard all day, while farther and higher up the road it melted after ten o'clock in the morning.

Our drive to the station was much more pleasant than the one to the farm on the night of the twenty-sixth. We started at half after one o'clock, in the same double wagon. As on our first trip, the Androscoggin was not fordable, and we had to drive far up the valley. Mount Washington, Boots Spur, and in fact the whole Presidential Range, were visible to their snow-clad summits; from the head of Mine Brook bridge the mountain view was superb.

After crossing the Androscoggin, we headed back down the valley under the shadow of Mount Winthrop, and passed the town pound. As the wagon rolled along I caught sight of two pine grosbeaks, who flew into some low trees. A few minutes later, far up on Mount Winthrop, we saw a large flock, climbing about the icy surface of Moses Ledge; one of the grosbeaks was climbing among the ice-bound hemlock boughs that had lodged half way down the ledge. I collected a specimen of this bird, and on examining the stomach *post mortem* I found in it, strange to say, small pieces of ice, — a means of getting water, no doubt. These were the first pine grosbeaks we had seen, and I believe that they had left the southern side of the valley and sought the northern and its cooler woods.

On reaching the station, we took the train, and soon left Shelburne, the mountains, the Androscoggin and the peaceful valley in possession of the hardy lumbermen.

V

WHERE FEBRUARY IS SPRING

IT is now well towards the end of March; the first bluebird and the robins and grackles have come, and while I am listening to the voices of many song sparrows from the thicket I seem to hear the voices I heard a month ago many miles to the southward in that land where February is spring. Near the boundary of the city of Washington, as I journeyed toward the Zoological Park on Rock Creek, on February 17th and 18th, now a month ago, a song sparrow was singing. They had been singing in that region for a week or two, and the voice was a pleasant reminder that spring opened with February there, although here in Massachusetts almost another moon awaited the sound of their chorus.

From the high bridge that spans Rock Creek I was able to get a magnificent view up the stream which ran tumbling over

ROCK CREEK

rock and log, twisting and turning between steep pine-clad hills toward the southeast. Such a stream with such beautiful environment should be clear as crystal, but this was not; it was muddy and tinged with reddish soil, over which it hurried. The woods for a mile or more along the eastern bank were of scrub (*Pinus virginiana*) and pitch pine (*Pinus rigida*), and it was while wandering leisurely through these evergreens that I met two new acquaintances, a tufted and a Carolina chickadee. They, too, were wandering along from tree to tree, searching every crevice in true Parus manner. The tufted, whose perky crest gave him a decidedly piquant air, kept in the upper branches and scolded at my presence in hoarse, angry tones, but the Carolinas drew near and called " Chicadeedee " with seeming indifference, as if I had not a better friend in the North by the same name. In fact, I had found a double of my best bird friend, and the discovery, in Dr. Hale's words, certainly " undid me." I was pleased, however, to learn that Parus

carolinensis had no such plaintive, sweet
"Phœbe" note as our blackcap, but that
he called "Phœbe-phœbe" in a hurried
and vulgar manner. I met a tufted later
in the day, and again next morning, when
he whistled his loud "Whi-oo-whi-oo-
whi-oo" as long as I remained within
hearing.

During my tramp I saw thousands of
crows, much more sociable than New
England crows. I could walk by or
under them but a few yards away without
having them flap off; and in the genus
Corvus I made another discovery of a
new friend, for the woods resounded with
the hoarse, young-crow-like calls of the
fish crow, and it was only occasionally I
heard the good, loud, respectable caw of
our northern bird. But otherwise the
two species, as far as appearances were
concerned, all went under the title of
simply crows. One is always glad to see
a familiar face or hear a voice he recog-
nizes among strangers. Thus I felt toward
the juncos and tree sparrows who greeted
me on all sides with their familiar song
— I heard them above all other strange
voices. Bobbing and skulking over and

under rock and log, I caught sight of a winter wren. He had claimed an offshoot brook of the creek, and alone he had remained in winter quarters. As I passed his domain he sang a snatch from his song, and all the woods looked green.

I left the creek where a stone bridge crossed it, and from a back garden of a tumble-down house I heard a song that I recognized as belonging to a bird I had once heard trying to lift his voice above the tumult of songs in a city bird store. A pair of cardinals were sole proprietors of this deserted garden, and they were worthy of a garden to themselves. One's eyes, in the North, are rarely filled with such an animated bit of color, and the song was worth a long walk to hear. About the old house and bridge, bird-life seemed to centre. Tree sparrows were singing softly as they bathed in an overflowed hollow and a single white-throat scarcely lifted his own song above his breath; nevertheless, he was to me a bit of Maine grafted into the South. I heard a faint scratching beneath a mountain laurel (*Kalmia latifolia*) thicket and stooping to look for the performer, hoping to find a fox sparrow, I heard above my head from the lower limbs of an overhanging beech tree a loud ringing song, followed by a shower of bird epithets. This burst of sound proceeded from two Carolina wrens who, with perpendicular tails and bowing heads, were bouncing about above me. They had all the bearing of the wren I had left down the creek and of the house and marsh wrens I am on such good terms with here, but they were something more of an opera-glass and decidedly more, of an ear-full.

Can winter still have Massachusetts within its grasp? I said to myself on the morning of February 18th, when I left the cars at Chevy Chase, Maryland, and set out over the rolling hills, where from every side I was greeted by the voices of many song sparrows. The thought had hardly crossed my mind when the soft, sweet notes of a bluebird fell like a benediction on my ears. No, not of one bluebird, but of fifty, for a flock were coming toward me out of the gray sky, and not until they had faded in the distance and the last note had died from my ears did I cease to strain my eyes toward the blessed country to which they were carrying tidings of spring. I have not seen such a flock since the direful Southern blizzard of 1895. Hope filled me for the future generations of bluebirds.

From the opposite crest of a hill the whistle of wings again drew my attention to earth. A flock of mourning doves were disappearing with wonderful rapidity. They regained their feeding ground while I tramped over other hills, for I flushed them again on my return.
In the valleys between the hills, where generally a brook flowed among a tangle of blackberry and scrub, I met another pair of cardinals, a tufted tit, hundreds of song and tree sparrows, besides a single fox sparrow. Crows, the greater percentage fish crows, were always in sight, but my new and rather uncouth friends of the morning, — for they came near enough to be called friends, — I saw only occasionally. The first was a turkey buzzard, — for no particular reason so far as I can see, a rare bird in southern New England, — who sat perched on a dead limb and as I approached stretched his wings above

his back, and not until I had drawn quite near did he fly. His white bill made an excellent field mark. It was just before returning to the city, when I was following up a motley flock of song, fox and tree sparrows and juncos along the edge of a clearing, that I saw what I took to be a black vulture coming toward me, and as he passed I could see that his bill and head were black. Off and on through the morning I would see a buzzard sailing with tilting V-shaped wings far above the trees.

How quickly my two mornings in those "fresh woods and pastures new" passed and when I returned to Massachusetts' February snow-bound woods I felt as if I had taken a step backward; a step into the past. At first I felt as if the edge had been taken off the surprises of the coming spring, but with the arrival within our borders of many of my February friends came the memory of that earlier spring and of those new bird-friends whom I hope soon to meet again.

AMERICAN ROBIN (from painting).

VI

FAMILIAR AND UNFAMILIAR BIRD SONGS

WHENEVER I hear a bird lift his free, wild voice in pasture or wood, I thank Heaven that there is no such personality as a singing teacher among birds to mechanicalize bird voices, to make their songs more finished, and that the Creator alone rules their hymns of praise.

Could I picture to you who have never listened, in words that would half express the sense of the delight, the peace, the charm of listening in some corner of hallowed Nature to simply the song of a bird, I would willingly do so, but alas! I cannot, and must hope that from my descriptions, poor as they are, you will seek to hear for yourselves the songs that have so charmed me and which from their loveliness defy expression and interpretation.

In "Summer Studies of Birds and Books" by W. Warde Fowler, there is an extremely interesting chapter " On the

Songs of Birds," thoroughly worth any one's reading. In one place he says, and only too truly, that bird songs cannot be written on music paper. To quote his very words "A poet can be translated from his own language into another with some show of success; but to write the song of a robin[1] on a musical stave is in my opinion not only to translate him but to traduce him." Then he goes on to say: "There is a very plain reason why all such attempts should be futile. The birds use no fixed intervals such as those in our artificial scale; their voices are wholly free and unfettered by convention, and they can make free use of any of the infinite number of intervals which in reality exist between one of our tones and another." It was only a day or two ago I saw a person with a note book with musical staves pasted in on which the songs of birds heard in the field were to be written. If we wish to put in black and white, for others' benefit, bird voices, we must satisfy ourselves by expressing their songs in words, without any attempt at musical description. In a few cases

[1] English robin.

certain combinations of letters will convey some idea of their notes, as for example the pleasant call of our titmouse, " chic-a-dee-dee." But we do not want to write these songs in a book; to get the full beauty of them we must impress them upon our minds by hearing them often, and then when we wish to recall them we may, with all their environment, which is half their charm, and no matter where we are we can hear our favorite bird singing his sweetest strain in some secluded spot we love.

There are two kinds of songs of which I would speak, familiar and unfamiliar.

February has hardly fairly retreated before we hear, each year, if we wander to some damp thicket of catbrier, blackberry and general underbrush, the low sweet voice of the song sparrow echoing from its depths, such a familiar voice and so joyously welcomed. Early in March whether the day be rainy or fair, if we chance to pass that way again we shall hear the song anew, sung instead from the uppermost spray of the thicket and its tones put new vigor into our winter-stricken bodies, give us a new lease of life as would

the Fountain of Youth if we could bathe in its limpid waters; and yet the little

singer asks nothing for his song, except the right to sing it unmolested to his better half and to his Maker. As the days grow longer we hear their voices in chorus from daybreak to twilight and our ears become indurated to their song, although more beautiful as the performers become enamored by the season, until we hear some individual bird reverse or vary his lay.

As the last ray of the golden sun fades in the sky of an April afternoon and the dusky afterglow is at hand, we listen to the evensong of the robins. Now from that low fence rail, now from the top of yonder tree comes the uncertain, often broken strain, though plaintive, exquisite and inspiring. It is an hour when the spirit of quietude and contentment rests on all and the song takes a peculiar hold upon us. We whisper,—

"Come to me, Robin! The daylight is dying,
Come to me now;
Come, ere the cypress-tree over me sighing,

Dank with the shadow-tide circles my brow;
Come, ere oblivion speed to me, flying
Swifter than thou!"

We lean our elbows on the gate and, with our chin between our palms, peer through the dusk to where the last songster is pouring forth in subdued notes the closing vesper. We wait for another repetition of those notes but all is still, save the "sleigh-bells" that echo from the marsh where the hyla sings.

We must step into Maine for a moment, although on the Birds' Highway during migration we hear it singing, to listen to the chant of another familiar bird, the white-throated sparrow. As we hearkened to the robins at sundown we will listen to the white-throats at sun-dawn. Perched on the top of a low spruce, bathed in 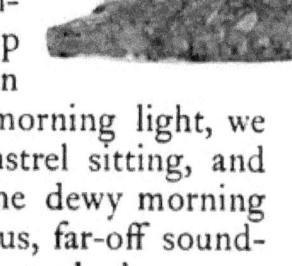 the first beams of the morning light, we shall find this little minstrel sitting, and hear wafted to us on the dewy morning air his plaintive, tremulous, far-off sounding "Pea-pea-peabody — peabody — peabody." And with the song, although it is July, will come some November and April pictures in which he was the central figure, and to me will also be brought the picture of a tall maple in a December snowstorm in Massachusetts with himself perched in the upper branches singing his sad refrain.

Before turning to study a quaint and curious master musician and to hear his unfamiliar song, we see a bobolink rise in ecstasy of joy from a bending dock, and as his hilarious, romping, ungovernable notes gushing out of his shaking throat reach our ears we find ourselves in many a meadow lounging in the delicious June sunshine among the waving timothy and drinking in the harmony that seems to bubble out of some spring above us in the ether.

How many of the sportsmen of eastern United States who consider the woodcock their favorite game bird and who have bagged many a brace, know of, or have listened to their love song. I think we could count them on our fingers. If we seek out a patch of low damp alder, with open stretches of meadow grass here and there where the woodcock loves to dwell, at the twilight hour at the close of a late March or early April day and seclude ourselves in some shadowy corner we may hear a curious note, sounding to different ears like "Nyah," "Peent," "Paap," — in fact apparently to everybody differently. A minute passes and we may catch sight of an object in the fading light spring into the air and while rising in long curves let fall a succession of musical notes; then the song changes and we realize that the bird is descending, the notes become more liquid and beautiful until the bird sinks again into the grass.

This flight-song is one of the most wonderful of bird utterances and surely we are wont to cry out to the bird as he springs upward again,

> "Teach me half the gladness
>   That thy brain must know,
> Such harmonious madness
>   From my lips would flow,
> The world should listen then, as I am listening
>   now?"

Think what voices are forever silenced each autumn by sportsmen! ah! I feel sure if each one of them could hear that song, fewer woodcock would fall to the lot of some faithful dog to retrieve. It is hardly a matter of prophecy, when we say that a quarter century will hear the last love song of the woodcock. It is an interesting fact that few of the early ornithologists heard it or were aware that Philohela minor possessed such a power.

When we know of an instance of an old Virginian having followed the singing of a northern shrike for an hour or more, supposing he was listening to the song of a mocking bird, we are praising the "butcher bird" in high terms. Nevertheless, such a thing has happened. We are surprised to find that Minot speaks of this bird as being "incapable of uttering musical sounds" and that Mr. Parkhurst in his "Bird Calendar" also writes in this wise — "a sort of miniature vulture in its habits and by one of the inexplicable mysteries of science classed among song birds! . . . My attention was first called to it by hearing a harsh, uncouth noise, as unmusical as the creaking of a hinge, which it somewhat resembled, but with a venomous touch of animosity. I never heard anything more barbaric from the throat of any bird, especially a 'song bird'; and according to all reports this was a fair exhibition of its musical ability." What a sad injustice both these writers have done the shrike. If Mr. Parkhurst had scanned the pages of Nuttall he would have found a glowing description of his powers. Even the female has a song. Here in Massachusetts in March and early April, or even as early as February, I have heard this "bloodthirsty villain" pour forth a beautiful, though disconnected song that would place him among some of our best songsters. He generally selects the top of some fairly lofty tree from which to sing his melody; in fact the shrike spends much of his time scanning the landscape from a convenient tree top. It seems strange that a bird of such tastes should be possessed of such a truly fine song, but even if he is a murderer, why should he not love at least a female of his own kin and try to win her with as much grace as many another bird?

While we are speaking of March songsters let us mention one more bird that comes to us in that windy month — the phœbe. His familiar " O-willy, o-will " has rung through too many orchards and

mingled too often with the rippling river to have escaped many ears — but comparatively few persons have seen him later in the season fly into the air and, while with rapid wing-beats he climbs the sky, utter his whole vocabulary of notes with praiseworthy gusto. It seems necessary for some birds to spring into the air and force out their music with all the energy in their little bodies, to express the joy that fills their overflowing souls.

Often entirely unnoticed and rarely observed, the brown creeper follows his monotonous spirals about tree trunk after tree trunk the day long, and perhaps this is the reason that so few of us have heard his exquisite song. Late in the spring, when the mild weather seems to have melted the winter out of his soul, he will sing to his accompanying mate, his wiry, sweet though feeble song, which you could not have believed would have issued from that demure bird with the sickle bill. He certainly sings as if his song were meant for a small audience, and surely only a small audience have ever listened to it.

There are few roamers of the woods who have not often heard a ringing " teacher - teacher - teacher - teacher " echo through their aisles and seen the chorister, the oven bird, walking sedately a horizontal bough. But if we remain in the wood till sundown is close at hand, we shall see him soar up through the trees, pouring forth an indescribable but beautiful song, until the night wraps the wood in shadow and silence.

And, last of all, the Maryland yellow-throat, who hides in the thicket with a black mask over his pert face, has beside his ventriloquous " wichety " which we know, generally long before we know himself, a musical achievement worthy of note. From the middle of May throughout the summer, when tired of the thicket's depths, he bursts its bonds and uttering an indescribable jingle climbs the air and then drops silently back again into its embrace.

Such songs as these seem to call out the good in a man and make him humble himself even before a bird, for surely he is without a soul who would not pause to listen to such divine melody.

AN OSPREY'S NEST.

VII

IN THE MOUNT HOPE LANDS

TO return to the place where one has spent almost every summer of one's life, though the time elapsed since the last departure has been only a few months, brings with each visit, new pleasures and surprises. Every landmark must be hunted up and every change noted. It is with the same pleasure now that I revisit certain spots in Bristol, Rhode Island, as when on returning to our summer cottage years ago I would ransack every drawer and closet to find some forgotten boyish toy of the previous season. Sometimes I wish I could live those summers over again, because I could spend them to better advantage, and yet those weeks from June to October when I lived in an atmosphere of do-nothingness I now deeply cherish. Bristol does not offer to outsiders the attractions it does to me, — they see only its surface, so to speak, — but each street of the old town and every bit of woodland on its outskirts has its notebook in my memory. At the station I am greeted by familiar faces and enjoy talking over the past severe winter (every

winter is severer than the last) with the proprietors of the different stores or farms. I know every one and every one knows me, and when there I dwell in a spirit of friendliness toward mankind in general.

My last visit was for three days, the nineteenth, twentieth and twenty-first of April, 1895. I arrived in the eight-o'clock

train from Boston, and was driven to my
"stopping-place," Mrs. ———'s, by a retired sea-captain in a rickety carryall, —
one of those delightful conveyances whose
front seat has to be tilted forward to allow
one to get in; and, no matter how well
you know it must be tilted back again for
your exit, you always endeavor to get out
beforehand. I occupied one of the back
rooms at Mrs. ———'s, which looked out
upon a decidedly primitive garden, whose
currant bushes were already in leaf, and
where one lone box-bush marked the
right angle of an extinct hedge. On my
left at the table sat Mrs. ———'s daughter,
Scylla, and it pleased me to imagine that
the name of Mrs. ———, who sat on my
right, might be Charybdis.

Shortly after arriving I started down
Hope Street out of the town, past the
Herreshoff Works, which have in the
past few years made this historic little
town more famous, and joined the Ferry
road. A fishhawk, the bird emblem of
Bristol, sailed over me "on his way a-fish-
ing" in Walker's Cove. From the meadows that stretch down to the bay the
plaintive whistle of the meadow lark

reached my ears, and as I climbed the stone wall and struck out across the fields, numerous cowbirds rose from the grass and sought a willow-shaded lane in advance of me.

Hog Island (every bay has its Hog Island) and Rhode Island itself lay toward the southwest, where the great fans of three old shingled windmills stood out against the sky. I followed the shore to the extreme point where Bristol Light is situated, and the keeper bemoaned, as did all those "along shore," the loss of some wharf or breakwater by the ice last winter. It is an interesting spot, Bristol Point. The channel, only a mile wide, is thirteen fathoms deep and the tide rushes in and out with great force. Coming from the Atlantic, sixteen miles away, and striving to reach Mount Hope Bay through this narrow gut, makes it one of the places dangerous to navigation in Narragansett Bay.

On the eastern side of the point, stretching back from a wall of low cliffs, is a patch of woods known as the "Junipers." This is now used as a cow pasture, and when rambling through the labyrinth of paths among the bay bushes one often meets a line of cows approaching in single file face to face. If their leader happens to be considerate of a wayfarer and breaks through the bushes to one side, well and good; but if they hold their ground, one must retreat to the first offshoot from the path or scramble out of the way into a tangle of brier and bush, a far from pleasant proceeding. Here crows are plentiful, and a "cotton-tail" disappearing in the underbrush is of common occurrence, but seldom is it more than a tail. The "Junipers" were more quiet than usual on those three days; the brown thrashers and cat-birds had not arrived, and cows and crows held undisputed sway. To follow the path along the cliff's edge meant seeing a kingfisher or two, while far out over the water a few gulls and fish-hawks sailed to and fro. At the northern end of the "Junipers" one emerges sharply into the pastures of an old Rhode Island farm, and the crossing of the stone wall that bounds the woods seems like stepping out of darkness into light. A flock of sheep browsed on the hillside, and a few white-bellied swallows circled over the farm buildings. From here to Mount Hope stretches lot after lot of farming land, dotted here and there with a house or barn.

In a few acres of bottom land I found a pair of vesper sparrows, and "red-wingers" as the farmers' boys call them, "quonk-a-reed" from every bush-top. Here in September and October fringed gentian is abundant, and in June blue flag and blue-eyed grass grow in profusion.

The osprey's nest is a decided characteristic of the Mount Hope lands, every farm having a pair of the birds either nesting in some decayed tree or on a pole on which the farmer has placed an old cart-wheel for their convenience. The ospreys return year after year in the first week in April and leave for the South when the gulls return.

It was not until the day after I arrived that I walked to Mount Hope and sought out King Philip's spring. Once having found the spring and seated myself near by, my thoughts pass back two hundred years and every stump becomes an Indian and the crackling of an approaching cow in the underbrush fills me for the moment with strange awe. Who can blame Philip for loving dearly that fair Rhode Island country? When there amid its loveliness I always feel deeply for him and his noble tribe who died in its defence.

On the further side of the mount is the Norseman's Rock, whose face bears, at least to me, an unreadable inscription. The view from the summit of the mount is fair, not bold; but my eyes never rested on one more lovely. It is "a matchless panorama of verdant fields, of waving forests and of sparkling waters." The rock that marks the highest point is only two hundred feet above the bay. A mountain climber would sneer at it; but it was named Montaup, and is to-day Mount Hope; so let it remain.

From two willows, near a pond on the side of an old road, on the morning of the twentieth, two goldfinches were singing; one was clad almost in summer garb, while the other had not lost his winter coat. Cowbirds were here in numbers, and a flicker had taken possession of a hole under the eaves of a summer cottage. The only chipping sparrow that I heard, sang every morning in Mrs. —— 's garden, and a song sparrow had taken up his dwelling there also. In the woodlands I heard the peculiar song of the yellow-rumped warblers, and at various times during my stay chickadees were noted. Once when strolling through the DeWolf woods I caught sight of a chickadee disappearing into a hole in a decayed birch. I approached quietly and clapped my hand over the entrance, thinking I had imprisoned him, when from above my head sounded a saucy " chic-a-dee," which I translated, " You haven't got me," — but when and how he got there I do not yet know.

At half after six o'clock on the morning of the twentieth I walked down the street where my hostess lived to the shore, and sat on a boulder looking out over the placid bay toward Pappoose-squaw, the sister point to Bristol, when a flock of nine wild geese passed over, flying east; they were so low that even the sound of their wings was audible. How calm and soothing the mild southwest breeze was; no such zephyr ever finds its way to the " north shore."

Late Friday afternoon I was driven to the station by the same retired sea-captain, and, as Mr. Bolles aptly described travelling by train in Cape Breton, as I sped toward Providence " names became places and then faded back to names again " until the setting of the sun beyond Greenwich shut out the passing panorama.

VIII

UNDER THE SHADOW OF WACHUSETT

UNDER the shadow of Wachusett Mountain, on the west, lies the little township of Hubbardston, Massachusetts, with its rolling hills and chain of stumpy picturesque ponds. The shadbush's fruit was falling and the mountain laurel's glory had passed when I visited in mid-July one of the farms on the old Westminster Road. Worcester County is ornithologically one of the most interesting spots in Massachusetts, and I looked forward to seeing and meeting many interesting bird acquaintances during my short stay. I had against me, of course, the season, — well advanced summer.

About the farm proper perhaps the chimney swift was the most common bird, and barn and tree swallows sat in long rows on the telephone wire or circled about the buildings. A pair of robins had their nest on a piazza-post near where

MOUNT WACHUSETT.

UNDER SHADOW OF WACHUSETT 81

a phœbe lived last year and another female I found brooding on a nest in an eye-beam under a wood shed. A few song and Savannah sparrows sang in the adjoining meadow where a flock of sheep browsed, and a chipping sparrow's nest was in the Virginia creeper on the piazza railing. A least flycatcher guarded the driveway trees.

I had seen one lone cliff swallow near the farm, and so during a long drive on the lovely undulating woodland roads that every now and then bring one suddenly out upon a deserted or tumble-down farmhouse with its overshadowing barn, I kept a look-out for their nests under the eaves. Only one nest with a brooding bird rewarded me, although I passed a dozen or more such unpainted, windowless, typical New England structures.

As we rumbled along, from the cool pine woods, black-throated green warblers could be heard above the noise of the wheels and squeaking whiffle-tree. A black-billed cuckoo crossed the road ahead of us into a patch of birches. By a rocky bare hilltop a bob-white was calling. Kingbirds quarrelled as they tumbled overhead on wing. A phœbe sat motionless on the ridge pole of a roadside shed. Bobolinks rose singing from an unmowed hay field. Goldfinches swung down the road before us and vesper sparrows dropped over the walls into the meadows. Red-eyed vireos sang on every hand. We stopped at an old unshingled house and I got down for a stroll. Behind the orchard a pond, which through the kindness of Uncle Sam had been stocked with German carp, lay among birches and pines. The big fish came to the surface to be fed with bread from the hand. About the pond circled three night hawks; a Maryland yellow-throat was singing down the brook, and out of a thicket where meadowsweet and fire-weed grew a catbird poured his soliloquy. Of a sudden the plaintive song of a white-throated sparrow drifted down from a pine hill. This species as a breeding bird is one of Worcester County's eccentricities. That single song was the spice of my entire ornithological trip. An American bittern with slow and stealthy stride was threading his way across a bit of low meadow just over the wall along the old Princeton-Gardner road. His yellow legs were sharply defined against the dark, dank grass.

As the sun was setting and tingeing the lily-padded waters of the Meadowbrook pond with its blush, I wandered down the road and put out upon its placid waters in an old flat boat.  The pond is the most southerly of the chain of six, almost encircled by a high fringe of mixed growths; at one corner two wide fields stretch away to the farm. As I drifted out from among the yellow spatter-docks into the fragrance of the true pond-lilies at the far end of the pond, two night herons sailed out of the fading light. I paddled within a few yards of one perched on an old dead cedar stub. A veery rolled out his music from near where I embarked. Darkness began to obliterate the shore, and to frog music I left the shadowy pond. The moon that rose from behind Wachusett later stretched its long finger of yellow light across the water when the night was far advanced, making the lingering shadows more intense.

Far up the valley where Monadnock loomed above the lower hills I drove next morning, passed the other ponds, one particularly picturesque with its old water wheel and dam. I was to visit a mysterious cave, which, tradition has it, smugglers inhabited. Where a turn is made into the less frequented lane that leads to the cave a giant chestnut stands, fully two hundred and fifty years old and fourteen feet in circumference four feet above the ground. High up a precipitous slope which the top of the great pines hardly reach, the entrance of the cave runs down into solid rock. I backed down with a lantern between its dripping walls. My voice echoed strangely. The bottom of the cave was covered with water a foot deep. As the lantern would not penetrate the gloom I crawled back into daylight. I am not envious of cave-dwelling animals. A wood thrush sang in the distance and companies of black-throated green warblers piped their wheezy songs above in the giant pines.

The pond with its changing cloud effects and luxuriant foliage was the most enticing spot, and I sauntered along a winding path, over brook and between fruit-laden shad bushes, a-birding. A family of black and white creepers were in evidence and called incessantly; a female redstart darted about, an oven bird and a scarlet tanager made music, while a chestnut-sided or a Nashville warbler would now and then join in the chorus. Two marsh hawks chased each other in the sultry sky. A flicker shouted in the distance and a crow cast his flapping shadow on the mirrored surface of the pond. Far up on the hillside a blue jay cried. On the waving birches a gaudy redwing occasionally swung with the southerly wind. The fragrance of the sweet fern laded the summer air. Where an old log spanned a rushing brook, a shy chickadee peered and with a dreamy note seemed to silence all but a croaking bull frog. The spell remained unbroken until a purple finch warbled softly, up near an old cemetery, and a field sparrow sang. When one songster pipes up after one of those silent moments when all Nature seems dozing at midday, it is the signal for other voices. The field sparrow's trill had hardly died away before a chewink twanged his instrument and ran his scale, two passing cedar birds whined and a brown thrasher chucked.

Pushing out among the lilies and stumps in the flat-boat, a spotted sandpiper took a loop down the shore and a green heron "pucked" nasally as he flew low following the bank around the pond. At the south end of Meadow-brook Pond a small forest of dead trees protrudes above the water from one to fifteen feet high, and from one of the lowest of these a kingbird flew while his mate scolded and hovered above the boat. Paddling up, I was taken aback to find in the crotch of the stub, but a foot above water, their nest and in it three blotched eggs. As I left them to their lighthouse home I wished them well, but if they had left the land for safety I had misgivings whether their offspring would ever reach terra firma, for their first flight would have to be over fifty yards. A wild venture for a young king. A kingfisher seemed to agree with me as he flew over.

On the morning of July nineteenth I started on a seven-mile drive to the summit of Wachusett. The sky was overhung with dark rain-clouds as the horse trotted over the pond bridges leaving the farm. The roadside was gay with summer flowers; fire-weed, wood lilies, meadowsweet and steeple-bush caught the eye. Swallows circled about the old farms, cedar birds whined in the orchards and indigo birds sang incessantly from the young birches. Many vesper sparrows ran along the walls or sprang from under the horse's feet. Two wood-pewees inhabited a piece of burnt ground by the roadside and a mourning dove, a little farther on, lit for an instant in a dead apple-tree as I passed. The last hill was finally reached before taking the mountain road. Off in the valley lay between wooded shores Lake Wachusett, leaden under the gray clouds. Rounding a sharp turn in the road I began to ascend the mountain's timbered sides. Wild raspberry was in bloom all along the zigzag path. Robins flew out over the valley. A scarlet tanager and a red-eye were singing near timber line as, turning the last curve, the summit and the mountain house were reached. Two towhees sang continually during my entire stay on the bare rocky crest, and a junco, a breeding bird on Wachusett's summit, 2,480 feet above sea-level, sang his simple trill. A rift in the clouds transformed the nearer misty hills, lakes and ponds, but even Monadnock could not be seen on account of the heavy clouds which shut in and hung below the mountain around its base.

A Meadow Clearing

IX

A MEADOW CHRONICLE

"PLING-pling-pling-tweet-tweet-tweet-de-eei" poured from the topmost twig of an old apple-tree. The singer was a song sparrow, and he repeated his modest strain a number of times, and then, as if dissatisfied, almost exactly reversed it and sang, "Tweet-tweet-tweet-pling-pling-de-eei," with more emphasis than before, and suddenly dropped into the long grass below, out of which he once again sang softly, then silence reigned.

It was a typical July morning, quiet, still and peaceful. No sound was to be heard except the "zizzing" of the insects and the subdued song of the birds. There were two busy families astir, however, for from one of the neighboring apple-trees a pair of kingbirds had just safely guided four restless babies out into the wide, wide world, and an equally industrious pair of chipping sparrows had done the same.

The four young kingbirds were sitting side by side on the upper rail of a fence, while one of their parents — I could not tell whether father or mother — hovered over the neighboring meadow in search of some insect to fill their gaping yellow throats, now poising over the yellow patches of St. John's-wort, now flying with rapid wing-beats to the foot of the meadow, and disappearing among the stems of some "cat-o'-nine-tails" that had sprung up in the cellar of what was once an exceedingly small cottage or else a fisherman's hut. Perhaps you will think it a queer place for "nine-tails," but the bottom of the meadow was very spongy from some underground spring. In a moment the parent arose and flew to the fence, greeted by the chattering cries of the youngsters. In the end of its beak, which was opened to its widest extent, was held the orange-red fruit of the night-shade. To its poisonous qualities, if it has any, was not paid the slightest heed; but, alighting on the fence, the old bird commenced beating it to pieces, and delivered it in portions to the crowding, chattering young, who, without the slightest apprehension, swallowed eagerly each one his share.

Knowing neither their names nor sex, I numbered them No. 1, 2, 3, and 4, although after each scrabble for food I was never quite sure that they regained the same order. The male or female, whichever it might be, after the nightshade course of their breakfast, sought again the meadow, and after a wild chase managed to capture a small moth which went to No. 2. After this the parent disappeared toward the other end of the orchard, and the youngsters settled down to take a short nap, with one eye open, no doubt, for danger, and looking like four grayish puff balls. As the old kingbird did not again appear I turned my attention to the chippies.

These babies, also four in number, gave their loving parents even more trouble than did the young kings, for one never stayed in the same tree for five minutes, and one or more often followed the male or female about (both parents were present) begging for food. The brood kept up a continual "chippering," and by the amount of food given to each, their capacity must be enormous compared with their size. It was interesting to watch the parent seek the tree where one had been a moment before and see how anxiously she peered around uttering a sharp " chip," and then when the young rascal answered from the next tree, how quickly the old bird would dart off to give to the mite, who stood with quivering wings and open mouth to receive the wriggling grub. I could tell instantly the young chippies from the old birds, as their breasts were streaked with dusky brown.

A pair of goldfinches undulated over the meadow and stopped for a moment at the right angle of the wall among the rusty stalks of a clump of dock and the delicate flower heads of the yellow loosestrife. Yellow predominates in the meadow now, St. John's-wort, loosestrife, tansy, butter-and-eggs and mullen being the principal colorists.

In crossing the meadow a few days ago, the old chippies arose from the grass and proclaimed the whereabouts of a youngster by anxious manner and loud " chips." I hunted about the spot whence they had started, and in a moment found one of their babies, who, when I picked him up, never uttered a word, or rather note, but sat in my hand and complacently stared at me. He was a very uninteresting little fellow, without a word for himself, and entirely devoid of good looks. As his parents seemed so worried for his safety, I, after much difficulty, sat him on the lowest limb of a young elm, and left him crouched down, his toes buried in his breast feathers, and gazing vaguely up into the blue sky above.

A pair of Baltimore orioles had also all they could well attend to in a family of six young ones. Baltimore children are the worst cry-babies I know of; all day long they kept up a continual squawking for food. The untiring efforts of their parents seemed to be of no avail, the more they received the more they wanted, and I must say I was glad when one morning they had vanished from the neighborhood.

The tall grass in the meadow I had almost decided was not to be cut, but early one morning a mowing machine arrived, and the whole field was turned to desolation before its clattering knives. My yellow loosestrife, tansy, St. John's-wort, and steeple-bush fell with the rest, and the kingbird family seemed to miss its waving surface as much as I did. No more could they hover over it, catching an unlucky grasshopper or moth, but had to alight among the stubble to scare them up, when a wild chase ensued. No more could tiger swallow-tail or the little cabbage butterflies float over its fragrant grasses. The beauty of my meadow gone, my three families having almost deserted it, I turned my attention to other quarters, but the sweet voice of the little song sparrow was still to be heard pouring out his soul from the old apple-tree's crest.

Swallow Pond.

X

SWALLOW POND

EVERY lover of Nature has a certain spot to which he always wanders when a few hours, or even minutes, are granted him to pursue his studies of bird or flower. The few acres of country to which I have paid innumerable visits at all seasons of the year and under all conditions of weather, I know as the Swallow Pond region, and I feel to-day as if it almost belonged to me.

This bit of country, where Nature still holds sway, is composed of the wilder portions of three estates, and though diminutive in the extreme, it yet offers to the birds all the attractions of marsh, thicket, upland, orchard, and wood. In the eastern corner lies the pond itself, only some hundred feet in diameter, resembling an enormous bulb, its greater roots extending toward the west, in the form of two small and sluggish brooks. The very eastern boundary is marked by a line of white willows, while on its southern side is a "stumpy" cow pasture. Tall oaks, whose naked branches trace myriads of veins against the cold winter sunset, command the western and northern limits.

To the oaks and thickets in the winter comes the bold, northern shrike, and small troops of chickadees, downy woodpeckers, creepers and nuthatches, ransack the seven apple-trees I call my orchard. In marshes of this *rus in urbe* I find the first skunk cabbages, and in its meadows the first dandelions, buttercups, and daisies appear. The white willows, even in March, begin to show signs of life, and the red maples on the pond's bank turn fuzzy and misty at the death of winter.

Many an hour have I spent, sitting on the trunk of a fallen maple and watching the sojourning fox sparrows as they scratched among the underbrush, and listened to their glad song, which is the sweetest of the season. Here also from the swaying branches of a patch of alders the red-wings shout their "quonk-a-ree." Each spring a pair of kingfishers arrive in April at the pond, though what they find beyond a few horned pout (an uncommonly uninviting morsel) is more than I can see. They always disappear by the last week in May. Along the brook's side I am sure to find juncos and goldfinches, while flickers, crows, and blue jays are omnipresent the year round. In the last week in April, Savannah, vesper, field, and chipping sparrows arrive, and the sweet voice of the white-throated sparrow is to be continually heard through the spring. This year, for the first time, a pair of crows built in one of the white pines on the pond's edge, within one hundred feet of a great thoroughfare, a very exposed situation for Corvus to choose for his home. The chimney swifts inhabit the flues of a neighboring house, and can be seen darting in and out all summer. Barn and white-bellied swallows are also among the first spring arrivals, and circle over the fields and pond, often touching the latter's placid surface with their wing-tips.

One morning last May, when the night

before only a few scattered warblers were to be found, the whole migrating hosts of Mniotiltidae seemed to have arrived during the night; a single tree contained five different species. Following them from tree to bush they kept leading me from one spot to another until I became fairly bewildered by their overpowering numbers. Such days are never to be forgotten; the pleasure and excitement of that early morning ramble will linger long in my memory. If the birds would come only a species at a time as in March and even April, one could spend much more time with each individually, but when May has once set in and the main wave of migration has commenced, then every woodland, meadow and orchard is swarming with so many varieties that one is fairly overwhelmed.

In summer, night herons sit motionless on the dead limbs overhanging the water, and the kingfisher wakes the echoes with his loud rattle, and the lively solitary or spotted sandpiper paces the mud spots on the shore. The breezes carry the green carpet of duck-weed to the opposite banks of the pond, and numerous turtles sun themselves from every log.

In the meadows near by, the flower heads of the St. John's-wort become rusty. Butter-and-eggs are tall green steeples, with but a few flowers to grace their tops. Blue vervain is in bloom, and goldenrod proclaims the advent of autumn. A family of white-bellied nuthatches inhabited the region one summer. The resident flickers are driven from their apple-trees by companies of boys. Families of phœbes also survey the country from the dead limbs; they do not have to go far for insects in August. The delicate flowers of the touch-me-not waver in the gentle breeze, and mullein, self-heal and shepherd's purse are in abundance.

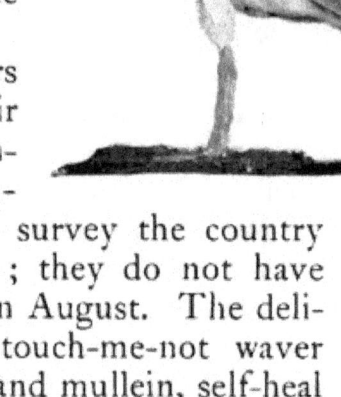

Summer gives a sombreness to Nature about the pond. The cries of the night heron at sundown add to the uncanny solitude. The outlines of the trees are lost as twilight falls, the wild noises of the night replace the singing of the insects, and the pond is bathed in the pale light of a midsummer's moon.

So on through the season this little spot of unspoiled country undergoes the changes of Nature. Winter with its snows, chickadees and shrikes; spring with its flowers, returning birds and budding trees; summer with its changing flora and warm still days, and autumn with its painted trees, goldenrod and departing birds. This place would have long ago been made public by having a street run through it, but on account of the impossibility of filling up the pond, as all the earth thrown in rapidly disappears, the scheme was abandoned. Let us hope the pond will retain its "unfillable" qualities, to coin a word, so that for many years to come it will remain "unimproved."

ISLESBOROUGH.

XI

IN THE LAND OF NORUMBEGA

This is the forest primeval. The murmuring pines and
 the hemlocks,
Bearded with moss, and in garments green, indistinct in
 the twilight,
Stand like Druids of eld, with voices sad and prophetic,
Stand like harpers hoar, with beards that rest on their
 bosoms.
Loud from its rocky caverns, the deep-voiced neighbor-
 ing ocean
Speaks, and in accents disconsolate answers the wail of
 the forest.
LONGFELLOW.

ON the south end of Islesborough, an island in the region called by tradition Norumbega, there lie about four hundred and fifty acres of woods. This tract is known as Pentagoët, the Indian name for Penobscot, and in the bay bearing this name Islesborough is situated. The view from the highest point, which is about one hundred feet above the sea, is very picturesque; spruce-covered islands with their serrated edges dot the bay, making it a characteristic scene of the Maine coast.

Far to the west the Camden Hills, Megunticook the highest, rising thirteen hundred and fifty feet above the level of the sea, form a mountainous background for the town of Camden itself that nestles down on the shore at their base. To the south lie the islands North Haven and Vinal Haven — the two together are called the Fox Islands; and many others too numerous to name divide the bay into many smaller bays and channels. This view is said to resemble strongly the English Lakes. The rugged gray slate-stone shores, the yellow tinge of the sea-weed at low tide, above them the dark green foliage of the spruces and now and then the lighter shades of a tall beech, with an occasional glimpse of a red-brown meadow, make the islands themselves beautiful.

Among the firs on the west side of the point facing the water is an interesting grave-yard of the early settlers. The dates on the headstones, which are either native slate or marble, go back as far as the year 1781, showing approximately how long ago the island was inhabited.

The larger birds first attract one's attention, and the most numerous of these in summer are the gulls, crows and fishhawks. The gulls as well as the fishhawks breed in large numbers on the island, and the cry of the osprey as he circles over the water for his prey is a familiar sound. A pair of chimney swifts evidently dwelt in the chimney of the house in which I was staying, as they were continually circling the sky with the barn swallows.

Juncos could be seen frequently; their plumage seemed duller since last I saw them as they passed through Massachusetts in the early spring on their way north. Chipping, song and white-throated sparrows inhabited the island, and I was surprised to see only three robins during my visit. On Saturday afternoon, August 4th, 1894, I wandered down the hill to the lowlands towards Pendleton's Point. Clumps of waving ferns grew around the rocks and boulders that were scattered through the rough fields, and red-thistles bristled from the grass. A sparrow-hawk flew off over the woods as I approached, and a fox sparrow took refuge in the depths of a dark spruce. The air was laden with the delicious odor of the balsam firs, sweet fern and wild roses; deep maroon cones hung on the branches of the spruce in striking contrast to the green limbs.

A field sparrow sang from some distant tree and a pair of kingbirds scolded as I drew near their domain. Two chickadees, a black poll warbler and a peabody bird hovered among the firs, not showing the slightest fear at my inspecting them so closely. Many half-dead trees were draped in long festoons of silvery moss. From the shores came the notes of spotted and least sandpipers, and from the woods the "flick, flick, flick" of a golden-winged woodpecker. Large flame-colored toadstools and fungi grew among the pine needles on the ground, and I could hear all day the tinkling of cow-bells from the fields behind the woods, like the sounds of the bells from the cattle grazing on the Swiss mountain sides. Two red-eyed vireos and a redstart fluttered through the birches and alders in a small patch of swampy land.

In the winter of 1893 a snowy owl was shot on this land, and eagles are also occasionally to be seen during the year. In the early morning, between sunrise and six, the sweet song of the white-throated sparrow could be heard; he is one of the finest songsters in the Maine woods, and as he stands on the top of a waving spruce and pours forth his song, who would not listen? This little minstrel often bears the proud title of "song thrush" here in his island home.

The backs of crabs and sea urchins I found in great numbers along the shores; the coloring of the latter was exquisite. Great blue and night heron could be seen standing at low tide in the water in search of the small fish that abound in the shallow inlets. I heard the soft whistle of a yellow-leg as he flew over the bay on the morning of August 5th, and the chattering of red squirrels broke the silence. The note of a golden-crowned kinglet came from the woods as

I drove down the island on the same morning. Soft white fleecy clouds drifting slowly across the sky made changing shadows on the Camden Hills and the dark forests of the many islands. Between North Haven and Mark Island you could catch a glimpse of the ocean, where numbers of coasting schooners pass on their way to and from the Grand Banks; some were near enough for one to distinguish their sails, while others were hull down in the distance.

The roadsides were already gilded with goldenrod, the first tear of summer, and wild raspberries grew in the fields and along the fences. On the southern side of the point I discovered a yellow-rump, black poll and pine warbler, as they were feeding in some ground juniper. The plumage of the yellow-rump was very brilliant, — so much so that he suggested an Audubon warbler. Bunch berries grew in thick patches in the fields and butter-and-eggs were also abundant. Numbers of seal could be seen at low tide on the exposed ledges. Their heads are very much like a dog's and their eyes have a soft, sad, indescribable expression. Whistle-wing ducks, known generally as "whistlers," were common in the bay, and a tern or two were about.

On the afternoon of Thursday, the 9th, as I sat on the upper deck of the little steamer Catherine, which threaded her way among the islands as she steamed toward Rockland, I looked back at Pentagoët as it lay under the heavy rain clouds of a northeast storm. It had been raining since the evening previous and the dark clouds had just begun to lighten, when, through a rift, the sun shot down, turning the Island, which a few minutes before had been gray and forbidding, into a glory of light and warmth, while the Camden Hills and the other neighboring islands remained the same, leaden and dull. In a few minutes we rounded the breakwater outside of Rockland Harbor, and Islesborough had passed from view.

XII

SUMMER BIRDS

A SENSE of stillness and peacefulness has stolen over the outdoor world, the foliage has attained its full luxuriousness, the lighter greens of the spring have turned darker and the summer sun shines down unmercifully upon man and bird.

We confine our rambles to the deep woods or along the beaches where we are fanned by ocean breezes. It is the season of recuperation for the birds after their housekeeping hardships and in view of their long migration journey, to begin before we are aware of it.

We rarely hear the wild wood ring with bird voices as we did a month or two ago, and if we do not tramp, tramp, tramp, — which beneath an August sun we never feel the least like doing, — our list of summer birds remains small; we must seek them in the shady nooks and corners if we wish to keep up old friendships.

A BEECH OPENING.

A wandering family may, however, visit the garden or orchard occasionally and give us a morning's pleasure in making their acquaintance, or an owl may take up his abode in our clump of pines for a fortnight and at sunset silhouette himself against the soft pink afterglow and whinnie mournfully at intervals till our blood stands still in our veins.

We may amuse ourselves, perhaps, by calling a bob-white and her covey within sight of the piazza or draw a company of screaming jays over your head with a "birch call." The dragonflies about the ponds, the butterflies in the meadows, the housing of the bees at twilight, the meeting of caterpillars on the footpath fill in the moments between the few birds we see on a ramble.

We broaden our studies more, we become botanists, entomologists, geologists, as well as ornithologists for the time being; we look into minor matters that during the migration and nesting season we had no time for. A longer pause is made to watch a soaring hawk or to examine a grasshopper's locomotive machinery.

In the latter part of July the bobolinks

cease to sing in the pasture lands and begin their roaming life. We may now and then find a stray loon or coot swimming on the mirrored bay, cripple birds, unable to migrate with their comrades in the spring. A flock of herring gulls often remain the year round in our waters dotting the rocks and sand-bars with their gray and silvery forms.

Summer days pass quickly by; we may have chanced to meet some birds when berrying, but our summer friends are old friends; we have a pleasant chat with each and wander on till the goldenrod whispers its same sad story of every year and the swallows that are flocking by thousands warn us that the great fall journey southward of the avian host has already commenced, and as the sun sinks in the last summer's sky we feel the cool September breeze sweep over the ripened fields.

> "Summer, sister, seraph,
> Let us go with thee!
> In the name of the bee,
> And of the butterfly,
> And of the breeze, amen!"

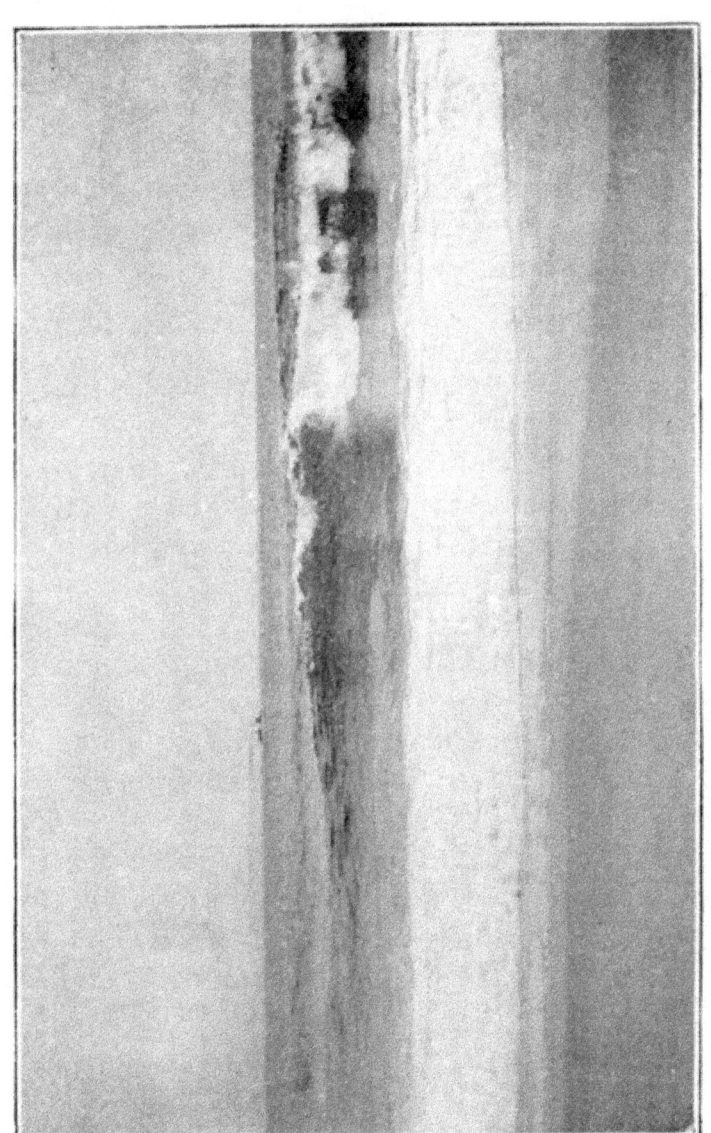

THE ATLANTIC.

XIII

ALONG THE BEACH

IT was early on the morning of July twenty-first, 1897, that I climbed with a friend into a two-seated wagon, bag and baggage, under the very eye of West Chop Light and started out on one of Martha's Vineyards old shell roads for the Katama Plains.

Our intention was a tramp *in quæsitu avium* around this great Massachusetts island, along the south or ocean beach from Katama to Gay Head, then back by the Vineyard Sound shore. It drizzled now and then as we set out, but the sun overpowered the gray clouds later and glistened on the shining foliage of the scrub oaks that compose the principal sylva of this island.

The avi-fauna of Martha's Vineyard is peculiar; few species, hundreds of individuals. Chewinks are omnipresent, and their song is the most continuous sound we heard. It echoes from the roadsides, from the woodland, from hill-top and valley. The brown thrasher seems to hold an equal share of the island's territory, — perhaps I can say terra firma, — while the pine and prairie warblers divide the tree-tops among themselves. I do

not mean to say that these four birds just named are alone on the uplands of the island. The black-throated green warblers, chickadees, Maryland yellow-throats, field sparrows, red-eyed vireos and vesper sparrows sang to us during our long drive, and blue jays, wood pewees, dainty hummers, swifts and song sparrows and the sociable chipping sparrows inhabited the immediate vicinity of the West Chop Light.

Our driver, an enormous man, who regaled us with reminiscences of his childhood, lived in the country through which our panting horse was slowly taking us. There was the school-house, to reach which he had toddled over a mile or more of lonesome road twice a day at the age of five. On the left was the farm of his nearest neighbor. "Dun know who lives there now," he drawled, — as if he were a century instead of thirty-four years old. After we had worn out the landscape and tales of his childhood, and the conversation was running low, I ventured to ask the weight of our charioteer, who so completely filled the front seat of the wagon as he sat half turned about with one eye to the horse and one to us. One draws near the heart of man when he leads him to speak of his own human power, and his face lit up as he said, " Wal, guess how much I do weigh." " Two hundred and seven," I said, after taking him in from head to foot. " One hundred and ninety " was my companion's guess. " Two hundred and sixty-five, and all muscle," was his proud reply. " And I have not found a man in five years who can pinch my leg."

If a marsh hawk had not sprung from a dead stub and sailed away, I do not believe we would have ever begun our tramp.

After rumbling through the fields of the

few Katama farms, taking down and putting up fence bars at frequent intervals, we reached the shore of Herring Pond. There we unlimbered our truck, and, saying farewell to our driver and the freshly mown fields of hay, teaming with grackles and red-wing blackbirds we crossed a salt marsh to the beach dunes, which lay between the chain of brackish ponds that back the beach and the ocean.

Two night heron and a kingfisher sprang from the pond's edge as we started along the sandy beach. 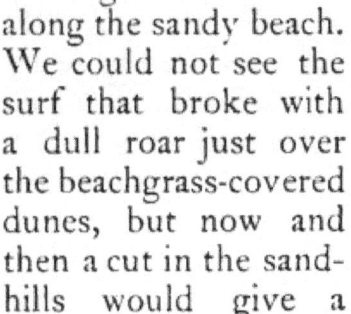 We could not see the surf that broke with a dull roar just over the beachgrass-covered dunes, but now and then a cut in the sandhills would give a glimpse of the wide-stretching waters of the Atlantic with a coasting schooner or two far out on its waters. How very small and insignificant one feels standing before such a waste of waters, symbolic of such unbounded power! Yonder wreck raises but a few gaunt ribs to speak of a vain battle against the waves.

> "The middle sea contains no crimson dulse,
> Its deeper waves cast up no pearls to view;
> Along the shore my hand is on its pulse,
> And I converse with many a shipwrecked crew."
>   THOREAU.

A single herring gull would sweep by over our heads out to sea or a few roseate or Wilson's terns would keep us company down the beach with slow wing-beats.

Spotted sandpipers were continually flushed at a few hundred yards apart all the way to Gay Head. Crows would blow up from behind the dunes where they had been feeding on the bounty of the ocean and sail off over the great surface of the inland waters. As we drew near the end of Herring Pond and entered a stretch of salt marsh a kingbird hovered over the waving grass and barn swallows caught many a gnat as they whirled against or glided down the wind. A song sparrow too sang from the remnant of an old fence.

Job's Neck Pond was link two in the chain and a few least terns that seemed to depend upon it for their food at once gave it notoriety in the notebook. Two little fluffy piping plover led us up the narrow beach; one at last sought refuge, when tired out, by squatting in the sand. "A fine example of protective coloration," I thought, as I tried to separate it from the pebbles and sand. Its brother or sister, whichever it was, a wonder at running,

scampered off over the dunes, doubling on our trail. We soon reached the usual bit of marsh separating each pond, and here I jotted down two laughing gulls that flapped over on the geological map we carried.

From among the tall salt grass on the edge of Faqua, the next pond, we started a sharp-tailed sparrow. Each pond seemed to be marked by some interesting bird, for in the little cove in the southern corner of Oyster Pond stood a winter yellow-leg almost up to his feathers in water.

This autumnal expectation and chance of meeting new bird friends drove away the monotony of the long chain of ponds and great curve of beach and undulating dunes.

The afternoon was well on when we rounded Homer Pond, having passed Watcha and its many tributaries and headed inland across a waste of marsh toward a little red shooting hut near the head of Long Cove. We found the camp and its contents exactly as our herculean driver of the morning had described it, and after a meagre supper we stretched ourselves full length upon the grass on a little hill back of the hut and watched the sunset to the distant drum music of the breaking waves.

Those two cool hours stretched on the grass were restful to mind and body after our long trudge over the hot sand and mosquito and gnat inhabited marsh. I drank in the plaintive whistle of a lone meadow lark up in the field, and the continuous undertone of grasshopper sparrow music,—that tinkling of tiny bells, —made one dreamy. A vesper sparrow sang from the hut's roof his degraded song-sparrow melody, and then as a flock of summer yellow-legs swung into the mud flats of Long Cove a chorus of sweet clear whistles drifted with the salt ocean air to us. It was an evening of peace. Peering into the darkness before closing the door on the sleeping land and restless waters, a trio of night heron cast their slow-moving shadows on the silvery flats of the starlit cove.

The sun had scarce risen above the eastern dunes when we resumed our tramp for Gay Head. Our path lay along the shores of Great Tisbury, Black Point, and Chilmark Ponds and over the Nashaquitsa cliffs. The same birds of the previous day accompanied us or appeared from time to time, but on a stretch of broad sand that separates the Atlantic from the Black Point waters we began to discover a number of least tern flying above us with their larger cousins. All the way to the cliffs a dozen or more birds would be in sight when one would look up and the easily distinguishable notes would continually be heard above those of the other species. On that stretch of sand three piping plover roamed and whistled their pleading notes.

A wood thrush could not sing against the roar of waves, but such delicious notes as the piping plover calls seem to blend perfectly with the uproar. Here on this tide-worn beach we saw our first flock of ringnecks flying in a compact mass along the pond's edge. Against the roofs and steeples of Tisbury, far back among the distant trees, a long line of black ducks swept past us while a few of the braver ones dived and scattered in Chilmark Pond.

We found a single egg in its sandy nest, but as there were both least tern and piping plover in the air absolute identification was impossible.

Where the cliffs first begin to rise from the dunes they are composed of the varied colored clays which give Gay Head its name and fame. Great flocks of sheep roamed the uplands; robins took the place of sandpipers, while white-breasted bank swallows and red-wing blackbirds were in the air instead of terns. Just before we reached a farmhouse at which our midday meal was to be secured, a patriarch marsh hawk was added to our morning's list. Beyond this hawk, Nashaquitsa Pond was, in a bird way, but a repetition of the many others.

A thunder-shower had hardly passed over and the rain was still falling when we set out again on our journey to Gay Head, then but four miles distant. The old Indian road was over undulating hills with miniature forests of bay bushes and general wild shrubbery on either hand and wood lilies brightened the path. On the right lay Menemsha Pond and beyond the bright Vineyard Sound and the Elisabeth Islands. To the left, across Nashaquitsa Pond, the ocean stretched to the horizon.

As we trudged along, new land birds were added to our list. Brown thrashers, catbirds and Maryland yellow-throats dodged in the thicket from time to time or sought some lofty spray to sing. The chewink was everywhere. Kingbirds that sat on the telegraph wires were joined by barn and tree swallows every second.

Vesper and song sparrows ran about in the dusty roads or slunk over the walls. Both roseate and Wilson's terns and often a stray laughing gull would pass over from pond to pond. When we crossed a rural bridge over Menemsha water red-wings were scolding and a kingfisher and a green heron moved restlessly about. A single Savanna sparrow drew my attention in the direction of a quaint tot of a yellow warbler; his parent also discovered him at the same instant, evidently much to her joy. Just before we overtook an Indian in a dilapidated carriage who was chatting to a neighbor by the roadside, three meadow larks settled down in a meadow with a laugh.

The now degenerate Indians of Gay Head are very hospitable people as long as one calls them Indians. But as about one per cent. of their blood now is Indian and the other ninety-nine per cent. negro, persons not accustomed to the correct human nomenclature of these people often find them an uncomfortable lot. This good Indian fisherman that we overtook gave us a lift in his wagon nearly to the great lighthouse, and, praising him on the brave work done by his people when the "Columbus" was wrecked, we were fast friends. The stern-piece bearing the name of that ill-fated steamer, lost below those colored cliffs on Devil's Bridge, he pointed out nailed above the door of an old shingled barn. His brother pulled an oar in one of the rescuing boats, he told us.

As we drove along, stopping now and then, while the Indian threw out a great weak fish by the road and hallooed to the occupants of a distant house to come and get it, a marsh hawk appeared and disappeared behind the rolling hills. Grackles were in the mown fields and three summer yellow-legs whistled in the distance.

Rain had set in in earnest when we reached the life-saving station, and as all the weather prophets foretold wet weather we cut short our tramp, left the north shore undiscovered, the heath hen for which the island is famous unsought-for, and boarded an excursion steamer for Vineyard Haven.

XIV

LATE SUMMER IN THE ADIRONDACKS

ON the very northern border of the Adirondacks, west of Lyon Mountain, Upper Chateaugay Lake stretches north and south between the surrounding hills. This wonderfully beautiful lake lies like a gentle maiden clasped in the wide-reaching arms of her wooer, the cloud-kissed mountain. As on the heart of a maiden is imprinted the face of her watchful lover, so on the lake's surface one sees, when her face is wrapped in serenity, the profile of the distant peak.

The whole picture looking out across the blue waters, over which a great bald eagle or an osprey might be soaring, was one of tranquillity. Above Bluff Point rises the crest of " Painter Hill" with its burnt forest to the north. Birch Hill, directly opposite, shuts out the ore-bed and the iron mine on Lyon Mountain's

THE CAMP AT THE SPRING.

ridge. Then the eye reaches the W. range; while behind, the Camp, Ragged, and Lookout mountains complete the encircling hills. Around Bluff Point run the narrows to the lower lake. Across the lake the East Inlet and the Owly-out, with their great sloughs, join with the greater water. At the head of the lake the South Inlet enters, coming from the spring far up through the alders. Wide-stretching sloughs of dead, standing, and fallen trees give companies of great blue heron and kingfishers a perfect paradise.

Under the shadow of a dark, moss-covered and sepulchral forest in a sheltered camp I spent late August and early September, 1897, a-birding. Life is worth living in such a spot. Some persons believe that one must get up with the sun at camp. A sunrise is a triumph of nature, but about once in two weeks throughout one's life is often enough to drink in its beauties. Everything becomes commonplace if seen daily. What cares the guide for the rising of the sun every dawn behind Lyon Mountain as he crosses the lake for the milk? The morning plunge was taken shortly before eight, when the blessed sun could warm with its vigorous rays one's shoulders while dressing, or, if the morning air were too chilly, a fire on the hearth took its place. Breakfast over, a little journey along the brook through the alders was always taken to see what the nightly migration had brought. One morning it might be a yellow-bellied flycatcher, another a shy water-thrush, while yet again one might miss the Connecticut warbler that chucked from a clump of underbrush the previous

morning. "The Alders," as they came to be called, was where one met the warbler and the vireo contingent in general, a stray pigeon hawk, an occasional downy or hairy woodpecker, a perfect congress of blue jays, a winter wren, a song sparrow, a golden-crowned kinglet, a nuthatch, or a wandering partridge from the deep forest. I recognized among the happy congregation of warblers that one met regularly passing through on their long journey, silent except for an occasional whisper, black-throated greens and blues, parulas, magnolias, blackburnians, Maryland yellow-throats and redstarts. Nashvilles, Canadians, black-polls, bay breasts, black and whites, chestnut-sideds, and oven birds one met less often. The loudest voice that 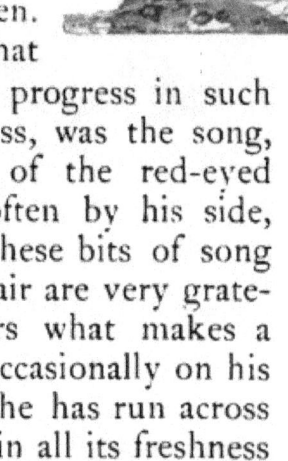 cheered this company's progress in such variety of autumnal dress, was the song, unchanged by season, of the red-eyed vireo. The solitary, often by his side, might pipe up too. These bits of song that warm the autumn air are very grateful — one often wonders what makes a warbler chance to sing occasionally on his autumn way — perhaps he has run across a leaf that in the spring in all its freshness had yielded up to him a peculiarly delicious grub. Man is delighted to find an old familiar landmark of long ago — why should not a bird be?

After going the round of "The Alders," we took a stroll to the spring, where a junco or two were greeted, and then up the path that led to "The Big Trees," two fathers of the forest, one still standing and the other prone. That sunless path was the sanctum of the thrushes. Hermits were all along the way and a big wood or demure olive-back might chance to peer at one from some great moss-covered log.

As we entered a blazed trail, perhaps leading to Mountain Pond or Ragged Lake, for a forenoon tramp, the stillness of the forest was delicious. Beneath those great trees, the pine, the hemlock, the balsam, the yellow birch, the spruce, moss-hung and stately, one was not alone. There was the little downy and his big cousin the hairy, within sight of the path perhaps, or drumming in the distance. A great crest might be heard calling his dreamy exhaust whistle. Through what a glory those paths led! The hobble bush, its red leaves and berries afire, stood by the way. The fruit of the trillium, bunchberry and jack-in-the-pulpit glowed amongst the ground hemlock. The corpse-like Indian pipe, lifting their tombstones on their heads, rose like ghosts from the soil. Clintonia borealis held its rich plum-colored fruit in air. It is the whole

luxuriance of a virgin forest — such a history of Nature's epochs that impresses one. Yonder great hemlock stub, punctured by the log cock, the pileated woodpecker, once ruler supreme of these northern forests, alone stands crying aloud, " Where is my persecutor? " " Almost exterminated," comes the answer; " one in that region to-day, where there were a score not long since." The ringing of the axe far up the valley, echoing from hill to hill, reveals only too plainly the cause. The blue jay that, down in " The Alders," practises his cousin's notes, is recognized as a close imitator, as the Canada jay calls from the monkey flower, his face besmeared with yellow stain.

The deep woods are always void of many birds — chipmunks and red squirrels seem to do most of the talking ; a chickadee may have just led one from the path, when, like a Fourth of July whistling bomb, a chipmunk will rush rattling up a log, and unless the chickadee pipes again he is forgotten.

The noonday sun creeps through the dense foliage when wandering homeward, and the "kip-kip" of a passing crossbill comes with it. Those single brilliant rays falling here upon a lichen-covered rock, or there over a fallen spruce, reveal the colorless shadows, bringing out exquisite detail.

There were six excursions I took from time to time, to the lake, inlets, sloughs, burnt ground, and to the spring. Each offered its own peculiar birds.

Just before sunset when the lake and its surrounding hills looked their loveliest I would take an Adirondack boat and row over its waters. A chimney swift, a tree swallow, a scattering of barn and a large company of cliff swallows during August would spend those best hours of the day with me on the lake. It was a pleasure to see the eave swallows in such evidence. With the smoke that drifted down from the mine furnaces would come a caw of a crow. He was a rare bird about the lake. A spotted or a semipalmated sandpiper one might find feeding on the protruding sand-bars; how far the ringneck plover that whistled from the sky seemed from his element near that untide-washed beach!

As the sun stole down in the sag of Hardwood Hill, a great change would take place in the lakes' and mountains' coloring. The waters would turn to molten silver, the hills into a leaden olive. With the chill of twilight, night hawks would come and with their crazy flight seem imitating the bats that dodged imaginary obstacles over the water near the shores. A teal might pump by, disappearing in a distant slough as one was rowing homeward. Late in the evening the quawk of a night heron would come in the cabin door. The guide, on his early morning row, saw a loon occasionally through the mist — he seemed to vanish, as it did under the sun's rays.

As one looks out upon the hills surrounding the lake, one sees here and there great patches of burnt ground. "Painter Hill" has such a one on its northern side. Far up behind the camp, a trail, running at right angles from the one leading to the "Big Trees," through tangles of wild raspberry, reaches a tract of ground, growing with little birches, great brakes and towering with gaunt trunks of the perished forest. There we found in the decayed mass of fallen trees the marks where "partridges" had been dusting themselves, and once flushed a bird. White-throated sparrows, juncos and vesper sparrows inhabited the underbrush, rose-breasted grosbeaks, scarlet tanagers, purple and gold finches, the birches and other low first growth, while stray bands of warblers would wander over the whole of the living foliage. The characteristic birds of the burnt ground, however, were the hawks, woodpeckers and flycatchers. A Cooper's, sharp shinned, or goshawk might be seen on the top of some dead stub. Sapsuckers and a single flicker one would surely find, and a wood pewee never failed to be trying to decide among the wealth of dead limbs which best suited his especial taste. Once, hearing a yellow-rumped warbler chucking violently as he flew over, I looked up and saw a mite of a humming bird vigorously chasing him toward the woods. At that time of year what offence could he have committed?

Toward the end of my visit, in September, with my host and guide, I started up the lake for a night at the spring. We left the guide to follow us with the provisions with orders to meet us at the dam for lunch. As we entered the slough at the head of the lake, a red-breasted merganser and a whistler flew out past us. Each bend in the inlet brought birds in view — it might be a sedate bronzed grackle wading along its shores, a catbird crying in the thicket, a black-billed cuckoo sitting over the crystal water, or some tall tree bending with a flock of cedar birds. Generally, however, it was a solitary sandpiper that sprang from the mud flat and disappeared calling around the next bend, or remained sitting without the slightest fear but a few feet off and eyed us. On one occasion a greater yellow-legs, seeming still more strangely out of place than did the ringneck and "peep" on the lake's beach, was standing in the black mud.

We met the guide at noon and ate our lunch on the spot where, a week before, we slept under our boat among the waving tamaracks. We began the second lap of our journey to the spring about half after two o'clock. I envied not the guide, whose boat was laden with camp supplies, pushing up through the alder-covered inlet to the spring.

After hiding our boat, we took to the trail on foot. Canada jays we met on the path, and hanging dead by the neck in a crotch of a bush I found an unlucky blue jay. No marks of shot were on his body, but his head was almost bald, covered with only pin feathers. He looked like a miniature vulture. I believe he died a natural death. Just toward twilight a Wilson's thrush sang twice.

We had hardly reached the log cabin

at the spring and stretched ourselves out upon its fragrant balsam bed, when the face of the good-natured guide was thrust in at the open door. " By Jolly, but that was a good pull," he said. He had performed the feat in about half the time we could have done it, and I do not believe he once relinquished the old clay pipe he held in his teeth.

We waded about in the spring, a stretch of water only some few inches deep, lying between the great overhanging trees of the forest, an exquisite spot, while the guide prepared supper. A colony of solitary sandpipers waded with us and a rusty grackle scolded. We found deer tracks of the night previous to and from an old lick.

It was nearly eight o'clock when, with the guide, gun, and lantern, I made my way down to the spring's edge. A root of a tree glowed with light as we passed. Placing the closed light on a pole, turned toward the long log, the deer lick across the spring, we waited silently. The moonlight shone down, gilding the water. It seemed so still, and yet we could hear so many noises. A mouse ran helter-skelter nearly over my foot. Bats flapped here and there across the moon-glade. The notes of hundreds of migrating birds were continually to be heard. A barred owl hooted twice far off in the woods —

adding to his regulation hoo-hoo — hoo, hoo, hoo, a long drawn out hoo-o-o-o-o that I thought at first was the whistle of the engine on the Chateaugay railroad far up the mountain's side. A red squirrel dropped bark on us from an overhanging limb. The stillness of the night seemed rather, as one listened, a babel of noises. Although, far off in the woods, at times we thought we heard a deer breaking underbrush on his way to the spring, none came in, so at twelve o'clock we stumbled back to camp. Mice had amused themselves by playing tag over my host's face every time he had tried to go to sleep, and had endeavored to carry off everything on the table. If they behaved thus after I had gone to sleep little I cared, for, rolled in my blanket on the delicious balsam bed after my long vigil, sleep was oh! so welcome.

Next morning we visited a tract of ground almost laid bare by the lumbermen and were much pleased to find, beside great flocks of robins and innumerable winter wrens in the underbrush, two American three-toed woodpeckers. Their notes are harsher than those of the hairy or sapsucker, which were also about, and one beat a tattoo on a dead tree loud enough to make a drummer boy green with envy. A broad-winged hawk was seen flying over the spring and a brace of woodcock were flushed from the alders where the inlet enters.

The last occupant of the camp had evidently had a little misunderstanding with a porcupine, for ceiling, walls, window, and floor were covered with his quills. That afternoon, as we left the foot of the inlet on our way homeward, two swamp sparrows were discovered in the grass on the slough's edge where the redwings dwell and a pigeon hawk was in command of the slough where but a day or two ago a red-shouldered hawk had held sway.

The evening preceding my departure

drew near and with it one of the most beautiful sunsets I have ever beheld. The atmosphere was as clear as crystal. To the top of Lyon Mountain seemed but a short walk. The lake's surface was an exquisite blue, dancing with light. Every hill stood out against its background, either mountain or sky, sharply defined. Instantaneously with the sky tingeing a faint pink, the water on the western shore began to turn leaden, while the little waves looked like mercury running over its surface. The west turned a deeper pink, the eastern sky a hazy purple. Slowly the dark waters crept across the lake and color rose upon the foothills. The west was red and the east becoming still more purple. The waters were turning roseate; the color seemed to run about as oil between the dying waves. The sun had sunk, yet still the mountain's crest was golden with its light. Long fingers of flame reached up behind the hill across the sky; mock fingers stretched across the lake. Then slowly the sun withdrew its grasp upon the scene, withdrew her outreached hand, turned down her golden eye from off the mountain's peak; all light had faded, all looked cold. Forms became mere outlines and the chill breath of evening whispered night; mist hung round. I felt, as I watched that sunset turning from warmth and light to chill and darkness, as if I were looking into the depths of some dying creature's eye, watching life fade and death creep in — the soul fleeting as the sun had sunk — until mist had shut out all light.

Appendix

Complete lists of the Birds observed at various localities where a number of the foregoing chapters were written.

BIRDS OF BRISTOL, RHODE ISLAND

Chapters II. and VII.

1. *Colymbus holbœllii* — Red-necked Grebe.
2. *Colymbus auritus* — Horned Grebe.
3. *Gavia imber* — Loon.
4. *Larus argentatus smithsonianus* — American Herring Gull.
5. *Sterna hirundo* — Wilson's Tern.
6. *Merganser serrator* — Red-breasted Merganser.
7. *Clangula clangula americana* — American Golden-eye.
8. *Oidemia americana* — American Scoter.
9. *Oidemia deglandi* — White-winged Scoter.
10. *Branta canadensis* — Canada Goose.

11. *Branta bernicla* — Brant.
12. *Ardea herodias* — Great Blue Heron.
13. *Ardea virescens* — Green Heron.
14. *Nycticorax nycticorax nævius* — Black-crowned Night Heron.
15. *Philohela minor* — American Woodcock.
16. *Ereunetes pusillus* — Semipalmated Sandpiper.
17. *Actitis macularia* — Spotted Sandpiper.
18. *Colinus virginianus* — Bob-white.
19. *Circus hudsonius* — Marsh Hawk.
20. *Buteo lineatus* — Red-shouldered Hawk.
21. *Pandion haliaëtus carolinensis* — Osprey.
22. *Megascops asio* — Screech Owl.
23. *Coccyzus erythrophthalmus* — Black-billed Cuckoo.
24. *Ceryle alcyon* — Belted Kingfisher.
25. *Dryobates pubescens medianus* — Downy Woodpecker.
26. *Sphyrapicus varius* — Yellow-bellied Sapsucker.
27. *Colaptes auratus luteus* — Northern Flicker.
28. *Chætura pelagica* — Chimney Swift.
29. *Trochilus colubris* — Ruby-throated Hummingbird.

APPENDIX

30. *Tyrannus tyrannus* — Kingbird.
31. *Myiarchus crinitus* — Crested Flycatcher.
32. *Sayornis phœbe* — Phœbe.
33. *Contopus virens* — Wood Pewee.
34. *Empidonax minimus* — Least Flycatcher.
35. *Cyanocitta cristata* — Blue Jay.
36. *Corvus americanus* — American Crow.
37. *Dolichonyx oryzivorus* — Bobolink.
38. *Molothrus ater* — Cowbird.
39. *Agelaius phœniceus* — Red-winged Blackbird.
40. *Sturnella magna* — Meadow Lark.
41. *Icterus galbula* — Baltimore Oriole.
42. *Scolecophagus carolinus* — Rusty Grackle.
43. *Quiscalus quiscula* (?) — Purple Grackle.
44. *Carpodacus purpureus* — Purple Finch.
45. *Passer domesticus* — English Sparrow.
46. *Loxia curvirostra minor* — American Crossbill.
47. *Astragalinus tristis* — American Goldfinch.
48. *Passerina nivalis* — Snowflake.
49. *Poœcetes gramineus* — Vesper Sparrow.
50. *Ammodromus sandwichensis savanna* — Savanna Sparrow.

APPENDIX

51. *Zonotrichia albicollis*—White-throated Sparrow.
52. *Spizella monticola* — Tree Sparrow.
53. *Spizella socialis* — Chipping Sparrow.
54. *Spizella pusilla* — Field Sparrow.
55. *Junco hiemalis* — Slate-colored Junco.
56. *Melospiza fasciata* — Song Sparrow.
57. *Passerella iliaca* — Fox Sparrow.
58. *Progne subis* — Purple Martin.
59. *Petrochelidon lunifrons* — Cliff Swallow.
60. *Hirundo erythrogastra* — Barn Swallow.
61. *Tachycineta bicolor* — Tree Swallow.
62. *Ampelis cedrorum* — Cedar Waxwing.
63. *Vireo olivaceus* — Red-eyed Vireo.
64. *Mniotilta varia* — Black-and-white Warbler.
65. *Compsothlypis americana usneæ* — Northern Parula Warbler.
66. *Dendroica æstiva* — Yellow Warbler.
67. *Dendroica coronata* — Myrtle Warbler.
68. *Geothlypis trichas* — Maryland Yellow-throat.
69. *Setophaga ruticilla* — American Redstart.
70. *Anthus pensilvanicus* — American Pipit.

APPENDIX

71. *Gaieoscoptes carolinensis* — Catbird.
72. *Harporhynchus rufus* — Brown Thrasher.
73. *Troglodytes aëdon* — House Wren.
74. *Certhia familiaris fusca* — Brown Creeper.
75. *Sitta carolinensis* — White-breasted Nuthatch.
76. *Parus atricapillus* — Chickadee.
77. *Regulus satrapa* — Golden-crowned Kinglet.
78. *Regulus calendula* — Ruby-crowned Kinglet.
79. *Hylocichla fuscescens* — Wilson's Thrush.
80. *Hylocichla aonalaschkæ pallasii* — Hermit Thrush.
81. *Merula migratoria* — American Robin.
82. *Sialia sialis* — Bluebird.

BIRDS OF WASHINGTON, D. C., AND CHEVY CHASE, MARYLAND

Chapter V.

1. *Larus argentatus smithsonianus* — American Herring Gull.
2. *Zenaidura macroura* — Mourning Dove.

3. *Cathartes aura* — Turkey Vulture.
4. *Cathartes uruba* — Black Vulture (?)
    The identification of this bird was practically positive without taking of specimen.
5. *Dryobates pubescens medianus* — Downy Woodpecker.
6. *Colaptes auratus luteus* — Northern Flicker.
7. *Corvus americanus* — American Crow.
8. *Corvus ossifragus* — Fish Crow.
9. *Quiscalus quiscula* — Purple Grackle.
10. *Poæcetes gramineus* — Vesper Sparrow.
11. *Zonotrichia albicollis* — White-throated Sparrow.
12. *Spizella monticola* — Tree Sparrow.
13. *Junco hiemalis* — Slate-colored Junco.
14. *Melospiza fasciata* — Song Sparrow.
15. *Passerella iliaca* — Fox Sparrow.
16. *Cardinalis cardinalis* — Cardinal.
17. *Thryothorus ludovicianus* — Carolina Wren.
18. *Anorthura hiemalis* — Winter Wren.
19. *Sitta carolinensis* — White-breasted Nuthatch.
20. *Sitta canadensis* — Red-breasted Nuthatch.
21. *Parus bicolor* — Tufted Titmouse.

APPENDIX

22. *Parus carolinensis* — Carolina Chickadee.
23. *Merula migratoria* — American Robin.
24. *Sialia sialis* — Bluebird.

BIRDS OF HUBBARDSTON, MASSACHUSETTS, AND VICINITY

CHAPTER VIII.

1. *Botaurus lentiginosus* — American Bittern.
2. *Ardea herodias* — Great Blue Heron.
3. *Ardea virescens* — Green Heron.
4. *Nycticorax nycticorax nævius* — Black-crowned Night Heron.
5. *Actitis macularia* — Spotted Sandpiper.
6. *Colinus virginianus* — Bob-white.
7. *Bonasa umbellus* — Ruffed Grouse.
8. *Zenaidura macroura* — Mourning Dove.
9. *Circus hudsonius* — Marsh Hawk.
10. *Coccyzus erythrophthalmus* — Black-billed Cuckoo.
11. *Ceryle alcyon* — Belted Kingfisher.
12. *Dryobates pubescens medianus* — Downy Woodpecker.

APPENDIX

13. *Colaptes auratus luteus* — Northern Flicker.
14. *Chordeilis virginianus* — Night Hawk.
15. *Chætura pelagica* — Chimney Swift.
16. *Trochilus colubris* — Ruby-throated Hummingbird.
17. *Tyrannus tyrannus* — Kingbird.
18. *Sayornis phœbe* — Phœbe.
19. *Contopus virens* — Wood Pewee.
20. *Empidonax minimus* — Least Flycatcher.
21. *Cyanocitta cristata* — Blue Jay.
22. *Corvus americanus* — American Crow.
23. *Dolichonyx oryzivorus* — Bobolink.
24. *Agelaius phæniceus* — Red-wing Blackbird.
25. *Sturnella magna* — Meadow Lark.
26. *Carpodacus purpureus* — Purple Finch.
27. *Astragalinus tristis* — American Goldfinch.
28. *Poæcetes gramineus* — Vesper Sparrow.
29. *Ammodromus sandwichensis savanna* — Savanna Sparrow.
30. *Zonotrichia albicollis* — White-throated Sparrow.
31. *Spizella socialis* — Chipping Sparrow.
32. *Spizella pusilla* — Field Sparrow.
33. *Junco hiemalis* — Slate-colored Junco.
34. *Melospiza fasciata* — Song Sparrow.

APPENDIX 161

35. *Pipilo erythrophthalmus* — Towhee.
36. *Passerina cyanea* — Indigo bird.
37. *Piranga erythromelas* — Scarlet Tanager.
38. *Petrochelidon lunifrons* — Cliff Swallow.
39. *Hirundo erythrogastra* — Barn Swallow.
40. *Tachycineta bicolor* — Tree Swallow.
41. *Ampelis cedrorum* — Cedar Waxwing.
42. *Vireo olivaceus* — Red-eyed Vireo.
43. *Mniotilta varia* — Black-and-white Warbler.
44. *Compsothlypis americana usneæ* — Northern Parula Warbler.
45. *Helminthophila rubricapilla* — Nashville Warbler.
46. *Dendroica pensylvanica* — Chestnut-sided Warbler.
47. *Dendroica virens* — Black-throated Green Warbler.
48. *Seiurus auricapillus* — Oven bird.
49. *Geothlypis trichas* — Maryland Yellowthroat.
50. *Setophaga ruticilla* — American Redstart.
51. *Galeoscoptes carolinensis* — Catbird.
52. *Harporhynchus rufus* — Brown Thrasher.
53. *Parus atricapillus* — Chickadee.
54. *Hylocichla mustelinus* — Wood Thrush.

55. *Hylocichla fuscescens* — Wilson's Thrush.
56. *Merula migratoria* — American Robin.

BIRDS OF CHATEAUGAY LAKE, NEW YORK
Chapter XIV

1. *Podylymbus podiceps* — Pied-billed Grebe.*
2. *Gavia imber* — Loon.
3. *Larus argentatus smithsonianus* — Herring Gull.*
4. *Merganser serrator* — Red-breasted Merganser (?)
5. *Lophodytes cucullatus* — Hooded Merganser.*
6. *Anas obscura* — Black Duck.
7. *Nettion carolinensis* — Green-winged Teal.
8. *Dafila acuta* — Pintail.* (?)
9. *Clangula clangula americana* — American Golden-eye.
10. *Oidemia perspicillata* — Surf Scoter.*
11. *Botaurus lentiginosus* — American Bittern.*
12. *Ardea herodias* — Great Blue Heron.
13. *Nycticorax nycticorax nævius* — Night Heron.

APPENDIX

14. *Philohela minor*—American Woodcock.
15. *Gallinago delicata* — Wilson's Snipe.*
16. *Tringa maculata*—Pectoral Sandpiper.*
17. *Tringa minutilla* — Least Sandpiper.*
18. *Ereunetes pusillus* — Semipalmated Sandpiper.
19. *Calidris arenaria* — Sanderling.*
20. *Totanus melanoleucus* — Greater Yellow-legs.
21. *Totanus flavipes*—Lesser Yellow-legs.*
22. *Helodromas solitarius*—Solitary Sandpiper.
23. *Actitis macularia*—Spotted Sandpiper.
24. *Charadrius dominicus* — American Golden Plover.*
25. *Ægialitis semipalmata* — Semipalmated Plover.
26. *Bonasa umbellus togata* — Canadian Ruffed Grouse.
27. *Circus hudsonius* — Marsh Hawk.*
28. *Accipiter velox*—Sharp-shinned Hawk.
29. *Accipiter cooperi* — Cooper's Hawk. (?)
30. *Accipiter atricapillus* — Goshawk.
31. *Buteo borealis* — Red-tailed Hawk.*
32. *Buteo lineatus* — Red-shouldered Hawk.
33. *Buteo latissimus* — Broad-winged Hawk.
34. *Haliæetus leucocephalus*— Bald Eagle.

35. *Falco columbarius* — Pigeon Hawk.
36. *Falco sparverius* — Sparrow Hawk.*
37. *Pandion haliaëtus carolinensis* — Osprey.
38. *Syrnium nebulosum* — Barred Owl.
39. *Megascops asio* — Screech Owl.*
40. *Coccyzus erythrophthalmus* — Black-billed Cuckoo.
41. *Ceryle alcyon* — Kingfisher.
42. *Dryobates villosus* — Hairy Woodpecker.
43. *Dryobates pubescens medianus* — Northern Downy Woodpecker.
44. *Picoides arcticus* — Arctic Three-toed Woodpecker.*
45. *Picoides americanus* — American Three-toed Woodpecker.
46. *Sphyrapicus varius* — Yellow-bellied Sapsucker.
47. *Ceophlœus pileatus* — Pileated Woodpecker.
48. *Colaptes auratus luteus* — Northern Flicker.
49. *Chordeiles virginianus* — Night Hawk.
50. *Chætura pelagica* — Chimney Swift.
51. *Trochilus colubris* — Ruby-throated Hummingbird.
52. *Tyrannus tyrannus* — Kingbird.
53. *Myiarchus crinitus* — Crested Flycatcher.

APPENDIX

54. *Contopus virens* — Wood Pewee.
55. *Empidonax flaviventris* — Yellow-bellied Flycatcher.
56. *Empidonax traillii alnorum* — Alder Flycatcher.*
57. *Empidonax minimus* — Least Flycatcher.*
58. *Cyanocitta cristata* — Blue Jay.
59. *Perisoreus canadensis* — Canada Jay.
60. *Corvus americanus* — American Crow.
61. *Agelaius phœniceus* — Red-winged Blackbird.
62. *Scolecophagus carolinus* — Rusty Grackle.
63. *Quiscalus quiscula auneus* — Bronzed Grackle.
64. *Carpodacus purpureus* — Purple Finch.
65. *Loxia curvirostra minor* — American Crossbill.
66. *Astragalinus tristis* — American Goldfinch.
67. *Poæcetes gramineus* — Vesper Sparrow.
row.
68. *Zonotrichia albicollis* — White-throated Sparrow.
69. *Spizella socialis* — Chipping Sparrow.
70. *Junco hiemalis* — Junco.
71. *Melospiza fasciata* — Song Sparrow.
72. *Melospiza georgiana* — Swamp Sparrow.

73. *Zamelodia ludoviciana* — Rose-breasted Grosbeak.
74. *Piranga erythromelas* — Scarlet Tanager.
75. *Petrochelidon lunifrons* — Cliff Swallow.
76. *Hirundo erythrogastra* — Barn Swallow.
77. *Tachycineta bicolor* — Tree Swallow.
78. *Clivicola riparia* — Bank Swallow.
79. *Ampelis cedrorum* — Cedar Waxwing.
80. *Vireo olivaceus* — Red-eyed Vireo.
81. *Vireo philadelphicus* — Philadelphia Vireo.
82. *Vireo flavifrons* — Yellow-throated Vireo.
83. *Vireo solitarius* — Solitary Vireo.
84. *Mniotilta varia* — Black and White Warbler.
85. *Helminthophila rubricapilla* — Nashville Warbler.
86. *Compsothlypis americana usneæ* — Northern Parula Warbler.
87. *Dendroica æstiva* — Yellow Warbler.
88. *Dendroica cærulescens* — Black-throated Blue Warbler.
89. *Dendroica coronata* — Myrtle Warbler.
90. *Dendroica maculosa* — Magnolia Warbler.

91. *Dendroica pensylvanica* — Chestnut-sided Warbler.
92. *Dendroica castanea* — Bay-breasted Warbler.
93. *Dendroica striata* — Black-poll Warbler.
94. *Dendroica blackburniæ* — Blackburnian Warbler.
95. *Dendroica virens* — Black-throated Green Warbler.
96. *Dendroica palmarum* (?) — Palm Warbler.
97. *Seiurus aurocapillus* — Oven bird.
98. *Seiurus noveboracensis* — Water Thrush.
99. *Geothlypis agilis* — Connecticut Warbler.
100. *Geothlypis philadelphia* — Mourning Warbler.
101. *Geothlypis trichas* — Maryland Yellow-throat.
102. *Setophaga ruticilla* — American Redstart.
103. *Wilsonia pusilla* — Wilson's Warbler.*
104. *Wilsonia canadensis* — Canadian Warbler.
105. *Anthus pensilvanicus* — American Pipit.

168   APPENDIX

106. *Galeoscoptes carolinensis* — Catbird.
107. *Anorthura hiemalis* — Winter Wren.
108. *Certhia familiaris fusca* — Brown Creeper.*
109. *Sitta carolinensis* — White-breasted Nuthatch.
110. *Sitta canadensis* — Red-bellied Nuthatch.
111. *Parus atricapillus* — Chickadee.
112. *Regulus satrapa* — Golden-crowned Kinglet.
113. *Regulus calendula* — Ruby-crowned Kinglet.*
114. *Hylocichla mustelinus* — Wood Thrush.
115. *Hylocichla fuscescens* — Wilson's Thrush.
116. *Hylocichla ustulatus swainsonii* — Olive-backed Thrush.
117. *Hylocichla aonalaschkæ pallasii* — Hermit Thrush.
118. *Merula migratoria* — American Robin.
119. *Sialia sialis* — Bluebird.

Names having an * after them are species that Mr. George C. Shattuck of Boston has kindly allowed me to add to this list, which are species he has observed during the past five years at Chateaugay, in addition to the species I had the pleasure of seeing with him in the autumn of 1897.

Index

Bittern, American, 83.
Bobolink, 60, 82, 117.
Bob-white, 5, 82, 117.
Blackbird, Red-winged, 74, 85, 100, 124, 129, 131.
Bluebird, 46, 50, 51.
Bunting, Snow, 8, 18, 23, 24, 25, 32, 33.
"Butcherbird," 62.
Buzzard, Turkey, 51, 52.
Catbird, 73, 82, 87, 130, 145.
Cardinal, 49, 51.
Cedarbird, 86, 145.
Chewink, 86, 121, 130.
Chickadee, 3, 4, 8, 15, 32, 35, 37, 38, 40, 76, 86, 100, 102, 110, 122, 142.
    Carolina, 47.
    Hudson Bay, 9, 35.
    Tufted, 47.
Coot, 17, 118.
Cowbird, 72, 75.
Creeper, Black and White, 85.
    Brown, 4, 7, 64, 100.
Crossbill, American, 9, 18, 32, 37, 38, 41, 142.

Crossbill, Red, 26, 35, 39.
> White-winged, 35.

Crow, American, 2, 5, 15, 24, 25, 29, 48, 51, 73, 85, 101, 109, 125, 143.
> Fish, 48, 51.

Cuckoo, Black-billed, 82, 145.
Dove, Mourning, 51, 88.
Duck, Black, 129.
Eagle, Bald, 111, 136.
Finch, Pine, 9, 144.
> Purple, 86.

Flicker, 6, 16, 25, 75, 85, 101, 102, 145.
Flycatcher, Crested, 140.
> Least, 81.
> Yellow-bellied, 138.

Goldfinch, American, 2, 9, 75, 82, 94, 101, 144.
Goose, Canada, 76.
Goshawk, American, 145.
Grackle, Bronzed, 46, 124, 132, 145.
> Rusty, 147.

Grebe, Horned, 17.
> Red-necked, 17.

Grosbeak, Rose-breasted, 144.
> Pine, 11, 42.

Grouse, Ruffed, 5, 38, 40.
Gull, Herring, 16, 23, 25, 29, 73, 109, 118, 125.
> Laughing, 126, 131.
> Winter, 17.

Heath Hen, 133.

Hawk, Broad-winged, 149.
    Cooper's, 145.
    Fish, 71, 73, 109.
    Marsh, 85, 123, 130, 132.
    Night, 82, 143.
    Pigeon, 138, 149.
    Red-shouldered, 4, 149.
    Sharp-shinned, 145.
    Sparrow, 110.
Heron, Black-crowned Night, 7, 84, 102, 111, 124, 125, 144.
    Great Blue, 111, 137.
    Green, 86, 131.
Hummingbird, Ruby-throated, 122, 145.
Indigo-bird, 87.
Jay, Blue, 4, 6, 37, 38, 41, 85, 101, 117, 122, 138, 142, 146.
    Canada, 36, 41, 142, 146.
Junco, Slate-colored, 9, 11, 48, 52, 88, 101, 109, 140, 144.
Kingbird, 82, 86, 91, 92, 93, 96, 110, 125, 130.
Kingfisher, Belted, 73, 87, 100, 102, 124, 131, 137.
Kinglet, Golden-crowned, 5, 37, 40, 111, 138.
Lark, Horned, 25.
    Meadow, 6, 24, 71, 127, 131.
    Shore, 8, 18, 23, 24.
Log Cock, 141.
Longspur, Lapland, 8.
Loon, 6, 17, 118, 144.

INDEX

Maryland Yellow-throat, 65, 82, 122, 130, 139.
Merganser, Red-breasted, 17, 40, 145.
Mockingbird, 9.
Moosebird, 6.
Nuthatch, Red-breasted, 32, 38, 39, 40.
    White-breasted, 4, 38, 39, 40, 100, 102, 139.
Oriole, Baltimore, 95.
Osprey, 74, 109, 136.
Ovenbird, 65, 85, 139.
Owl, Barred, 7, 148.
    Screech, 7.
    Short-eared, 18.
    Snowy, 18, 111.
"Partridge," 35, 38, 139, 144.
Peabodybird, 110.
Pewee, Wood, 88, 122, 145.
Phœbe, 64, 81, 82, 102.
Plover, Piping, 125, 129.
    Semipalmated, 129.
Redpoll, 9.
Redstart, American, 85, 110, 139.
Ringneck, 129, 143, 145.
Robin, American, 5, 46, 58, 59, 80, 88, 109, 129, 149.
    English, 56.
Sandpiper, Least, 110.
    Purple, 17.
    Semipalmated, 143.
    Solitary, 102, 145, 147.

Sandpiper, Spotted, 86, 102, 110, 125, 143.
Sapsucker, Yellow-bellied, 145, 149.
Shrike, Northern, 9, 62, 63, 100, 102.
Siskin, Pine, 9, 40.
Snowbird, 7.
Snowflake, 8.
Sparrow, Chipping, 76, 81, 91, 93, 94, 101, 109, 122.
    Field, 86, 101, 110, 122.
    Fox, 50, 51, 52, 100, 110.
    Grasshopper, 127.
    Ipswich, 25.
    Savanna, 81, 101, 131.
    Sharp-tailed, 126.
    Song, 3, 9, 11, 16, 46, 50, 51, 52, 57, 81, 91, 96, 109, 122, 125, 128, 131, 138.
    Swamp, 149.
    Tree, 8, 26, 48, 49, 51, 52.
    Vesper, 74, 82, 87, 101, 122, 128, 131, 144.
    White-throated, 49, 59, 82, 101, 109, 111, 144.
Swallow, Barn, 80, 101, 109, 125, 130, 143.
    Bank, 129.
    Cliff, 81, 143.
    Eave, 143.
    Tree, 80, 130, 143.
    White-bellied, 74, 101, 129.
Swift, Chimney, 80, 101, 109, 122, 143.

Tanager, Scarlet, 85, 88, 144.
Teal, Green-winged, 144.
Tern, Least, 125, 128, 129.
    Wilson's, 113, 125, 131.
    Roseate, 125, 131.
Titmouse, Tufted, 51.
Thrasher, Brown, 73, 86, 122, 130.
Thrush, Hermit, 140.
       Olive-backed, 140.
       Water 138.
       Wilson's, 146.
       Wood, 129, 140.
Towhee, 88.
Veery, 84.
Vireo, Red-eyed, 82, 88, 110, 122, 139.
    Solitary, 139.
Vulture, Black, 52.
Warbler, Audubon, 112.
       Bay-breasted, 139.
       Black and White, 139.
       Black-throated Blue, 139.
       Blackburnian, 139.
       Black-poll, 110, 112, 139.
       Black-throated Green, 82, 85, 122, 139.
       Canadian, 139.
       Chestnut-sided, 85, 139.
       Connecticut, 138.
       Magnolia, 139.
       Myrtle, 15, 18.

INDEX

Warbler, Nashville, 85, 139.
    Parula, 139.
    Pine, 112, 122.
    Prairie 122.
    Yellow, 131.
    Yellow-rumped, 6, 76, 112, 145.
Whistler, 113, 145.
Woodcock, American, 60, 62, 149.
Woodpecker, American Three-toed, 140.
    Downy, 4, 6, 38, 100, 138, 140.
    Golden-winged, 110.
    Hairy, 6, 38, 39, 138, 140, 149.
    Pileated, 141.
Wren, Carolina, 50.
    House, 50.
    Marsh, 50.
    Winter, 9, 49, 138, 149.
Yellow-legs, Greater, 11, 127, 146.
    Lesser, 11, 111, 128, 132.

www.ingramcontent.com/pod-product-compliance
Lightning Source LLC
Chambersburg PA
CBHW031438160426
43195CB00010BB/777